MINORITY NATIONS IN THE A
OF UNCERTAINTY

New Paths to National Emancipation and Empowerment

For thirty years, Alain-G. Gagnon has been one of the world's leading experts on federalism and multinational democracies. In *Minority Nations in the Age of Uncertainty*, he presents an articulate and accessible introduction to the ways in which minority nations have begun to empower themselves in a global environment that is increasingly hostile to national minorities.

Comparing conditions in Quebec, Catalonia, and Scotland, Gagnon offers six interrelated essays on national minorities, processes of accommodation, and autonomy and self-determination within a modern democratic context. Based on a long career of scholarly study and public engagement, he argues that self-determination for these "nations without states" is best achieved through intercultural engagement and negotiation within the federal system, rather than through independence movements.

Already translated into fifteen languages from the original French, *Minority Nations in the Age of Uncertainty* is an essential text on the theory of multinational federalism and the politics of minority nations.

ALAIN-G. GAGNON is a professor and the Canada Research Chair in Quebec and Canadian Studies in the Department of Political Science at the Université du Québec à Montréal. He is the author or editor of more than fifty books. His most recent works include the sixth edition of *Canadian Politics* (with James Bickerton), *Federalism, Citizenship, and Quebec* (with Raffaele Iacovino), and *Contemporary Canadian Federalism: Foundations, Traditions, Institutions*.

Minority Nations in the Age of Uncertainty

New Paths to National Emancipation and Empowerment

ALAIN-G. GAGNON

UNIVERSITY OF TORONTO PRESS
Toronto Buffalo London

© University of Toronto Press 2014
Toronto Buffalo London
www.utppublishing.com
Printed in the U.S.A.

ISBN 978-1-4426-4970-5 (cloth)
ISBN 978-1-4426-2703-1 (paper)

Printed on acid-free, 100% post-consumer recycled paper with
vegetable-based inks.

Library and Archives Canada Cataloguing in Publication

Gagnon, Alain-G. (Alain-Gustave), 1954–
[Âge des incertitudes. English]
Minority nations in the age of uncertainty : new paths to
national emancipation and empowerment / Alain-G. Gagnon.

Translation of: L'âge des incertitudes.
Includes bibliographical references and indexes.
ISBN 978-1-4426-4970-5 (bound). – ISBN 978-1-4426-2703-1 (pbk.)

1. Federal government.   2. Linguistic minorities.   3. Minorities – Political
aspects.   4. Citizenship – Québec (Province).   5. Federal-provincial
relations – Québec (Province).   6. Federal government – Canada.
I. Title.   II. Title: Âge des incertitudes. English.

JC355.G3413 2014   321.02   C2014-905158-1

University of Toronto Press acknowledges the financial assistance to its
publishing program of the Canada Council for the Arts and the Ontario Arts
Council, an agency of the Government of Ontario.

University of Toronto Press acknowledges the financial support of the
Government of Canada through the Canada Book Fund for its publishing
activities.

Contents

Foreword, by James Tully   vii

Acknowledgments   xi

Introduction: National Cultures, Democracy, and Legitimacy   3

1 Linguistic Diversity, Language Policy, and the Limits of Federal
Accommodation   16
   "Personal," "Territorial," and "Institutional" Bilingualism   18
   Language Regimes: The "Push and Pull" Dynamic   21
   Three Case Studies   26
      New Brunswick   28
      Nunavut   29
      Catalonia   30

2 New Challenges for Multinational States: Globalization and
Competing Citizenship Regimes   34
   Globalization   35
      *An Example of the Globalization's Impact: The Cotonou
         Agreement*   36
      Constructing Europe   37
   Competing Citizenship Regimes   38
      Recognizing and Revealing Political Communities   39
      Towards a Social State   42

3 The Pillars of Quebec's New Citizenship Regime: The Informal
Constitution and Interculturalism   44
   Deepening and Expanding the "Informal Constitution"   46
   *Interculturalism, Active Citizenship, and the New "Vivre-
      Ensemble"*   50

4 From Containment to Empowerment: Moving towards Positive
   Autonomy   55
      The (Im)Balance of Power   57
      Containment and Contentment   59
      Two Conflicting Paradigms   62
      Integration and Empowerment   66

5 Towards Multinational Federalism: Moving beyond the
   Integration-Accommodation Dyad   72
      *States Facing National Diversity: Between Territorial Autonomy
         and Containment   73*
      Integration, Accommodation, and Empowerment   76
      *Multinational Federalism as an Empowering Force for National
         Minorities   78*

6 Rethinking Intercommunal Relations in Canada   82
      Pactism   83
      Establishing and Promoting a Federal Culture   85
      Treaty Federalism   89

Conclusion: Embracing a New Politics of Dignity and Hospitality   94
      *Towards a New Emancipatory Politics in Multinational Polities:
         Moderation, Dignity, and Hospitality   96*
      The Principle of Moderation   96
      The Principle of Dignity   97
      The Principle of Hospitality   99

Appendix: The Dignity of Catalonia   101

Notes   105

Bibliography   131

Name Index   151

Subject Index   153

Foreword

Professor Alain-G. Gagnon has been studying and writing on minority nations within federal states for over thirty years. He is one of the leading and most-respected authorities on Quebec, Scotland, and Catalonia as minority nations within their respective federal states. He is a Quebec political scientist, a comparative political scientist, and a political theorist of nationalism and federalism. His research, teaching, support for graduate students, and public activities have deeply shaped the academic and public discourse in Quebec and the rest of Canada. Moreover, his comparative work has been influential internationally, especially in Scotland and Catalonia.

Minority Nations in the Age of Uncertainty: New Paths to National Emancipation and Empowerment was originally published in French. Gagnon has translated and edited it for this English edition. The main objective of this important and timely study is to suggest new paths by which members of minority nations may work towards emancipating and empowering themselves within the federations in which they coexist with other nations and partners of various kinds. He calls these federations "multinational federations" – a concept that he has helped to establish as a distinct type of federation. His argument is that members of minority nations should consider two complementary new paths towards multinational federalism in the contemporary context. First, they should work towards national emancipation – in the form of internal self-determination within the federation – by means of transforming the federation through negotiation so that it accommodates and helps to empower national emancipation. Second, they should work within the minority nation towards national self-empowerment by exercising their powers of self-determination through new modes of civic and intercultural participation in the public life of their nation.

Gagnon points out that this proposal of a dual strategy has little public support at the moment. The nationalist parties in Quebec, Scotland, and Catalonia are oriented to independence and the formation of new, non-federal nation states. They do not support efforts to renew federalism because they often fail and, if successful, they undermine support for independence. The main federalist parties turn away from federal reform and towards economic competitiveness in the global economy, austerity, and debt reduction – policies that tend to homogenize diverse federations and subordinate them to transnational trade law. They do not support such reform because they are opposed to it or because they think it is a slippery slope to independence, whether it succeeds or fails. Despite these trends, Gagnon acknowledges that there have been some steps towards multinational federalism in practice and towards an appreciation of multinational federalism as a just and stable form of political association in political theory and public discourse over the last couple of decades. However, he argues that these steps in practice and theory are a long way from full-fledged multinational federalism: that is, federations that recognize and accommodate national emancipation of minority nations and minority nations that exercise self-determining empowerment. The two strategies of this text are designed to set out new paths towards full-fledged multinational federalism in practice and theory in these uncertain circumstances.

Gagnon sets out several new paths for consideration and discussion. I will mention three very briefly. To move forward on transforming federations so they recognize and accommodate their member nations, he recommends reviving the idea that federations are constituted by pacts among their constituent members. In the Canadian case, there is a long history of conceiving Canada as a "compact federation." The provinces are said to have created the federation by means of a compact between the provinces and the federal government in 1867, and this way of thinking continues to inform several basic relations among provinces and the federal government. Gagnon suggests working on an analogous partnership compact between Quebec, as a minority nation, and the rest of Canada, as a majority nation. This is a fruitful idea. However, the question commonly raised against a two-nation formulation of the partners as the starting point is that it appears pre-emptively to misrecognize and homogenize the federal diversity of provinces, territories, First Nations, and minority communities that constitute the rest of Canada (and Quebec), as well as overriding the original compact among provinces. This concern is based on the principles of diverse multinational federalism that Gagnon presents and defends: all members subject to and affected by the compact should have an effective say in the negotiation. This basic requirement does not preclude such a pact, but, rather, renders it legitimate. As the Supreme Court of Canada argued in the *Reference re the Secession of Quebec* (1998), the participants of the federation first have to work up the forms of recognition and representation they entrust to carry out the negotiations and ratification of such a compact for it to be democratically and federally legitimate. It is a key insight of this kind of diverse federalism that all members of a federation are as attached to their communities (provinces, minority communities, first nations, etc.) as members of minority nations are to theirs.

Moreover, the Supreme Court also argued, in the spirit of the compact tradition, that all participants of a diverse federation have the right to initiate changes to the federation and other partners have the duty to listen and to enter into negotiations if certain conditions are met. This right and its correlative duty are based on the court's view of a federal constitution as a global system of laws for the continual reconciliation of diversity with unity by means of nonviolent negotiation and compromise by its members over time. This seems very similar to the kind of federalism Gagnon recommends. He also sees the tradition of treaty federalism between the First Nations and the Crown, while sui generis, as analogous to the tradition of compact federalism.

In addition, Gagnon suggests that the members of minority nations consider exercising fully the powers of internal self-determination they have under international law as the means of self-empowerment and positive autonomy within federalism. Among the ways he recommends is the empowerment of individuals and groups to engage in the public life of their nation through new citizenship regimes and expanded forms of intercultural dialogue and cooperation among religiously, culturally, and linguistically diverse citizens. Some of these activities are promoted by the minority nation governments and their regional and municipal governments. Many others are self-generated and self-organized community-based organizations, cooperatives, and networks organized around public goods: the environment, local food, indigenous-settler partnerships, overcoming racism, sexism, and discrimination against religious minorities and immigrants in everyday life, Idle No More, popular assemblies in Spain, and so on. These civil society networks of community-based organizations and grass-roots federalism are rapidly expanding features of Quebec, Scotland, and Catalonia, and of the federations of which they are members.

In a rarely discussed section of the *Reference re the Secession of Quebec*, the Supreme Court went out of its way to say that the Quebec people, and any other peoples within Canada, have the right to exercise fully their powers of internal self-determination and that Canada has the duty to recognize and accommodate it within its constitutional system of laws. Thus, this path of empowerment of a diverse people also supports the path of renewed federalism. The path of self-empowerment has also been taken up by indigenous peoples, whose right of internal self-determination was fought for and recognized in the United Nations Declaration of the Rights of Indigenous Peoples (2007), which Canada ratified in 2010, thereby contributing to the enhancement of multinational federalism around the world.

Another path Gagnon recommends is to foster a diverse, multinational "federal culture" throughout existing federations with multiple nations. This is the most important path since, as we have seen, the major impasse is that the dominant parties seek to avoid or escape the norms of diverse federalism. Gagnon discusses a number of principles, norms, practices, and ways of relating to one another in everyday life that, if enacted, bring a shared federal culture into being. The resulting convivial informal federal relationships, based on the principles of moderation, dignity, and hospitality, are the ground of healthy formal federal relationships.

I know of no one who has done more to foster such a federal culture in their research, teaching, and public engagement than Alain Gagnon.[1]

James Tully
Distinguished Professor of Political Science, Law,
Indigenous Governance, and Philosophy,
University of Victoria

---

1 Gagnon discusses new paths to multinational federalism further in Alain-G. Gagnon, "Empowerment through Different Means: Regionalism, Nationalism, and Federalism," *The Trudeau Foundation Papers* 4, 1 (2012), 56–87.

Acknowledgments

At one point, I considered entitling this book "Retour d'Espagne" in honour of Riopelle's superb painting. The countless hours that I spent admiring this modern masterpiece at the Thyssen-Bornemisza museum in Madrid in the spring of 2010 greatly informed the first iterations of what has now transformed into *Minority Nations in the Age of Uncertainty*. The chaotic nature of the painting evokes a series of reflections: Which among the mosaic of colours is the dominant one? What binds this patchwork of intersecting and cross-cutting images? What lies beyond the frame for the slashes of green, black, red, and yellow striking out from the corners and depth of the canvas? It is within this context and with Riopelle's painting as my muse that I sat down to write about diversity, nationalism, and pluralism at the dawn of the third millennium. Thus, I owe an initial debt of gratitude to Riopelle and "Retour d'Espagne."

I also wish to express my thanks to the Faculty of Law at l'Universidad Carlos III de Madrid, where I was most graciously hosted, under the auspices of the faculty's Banco Santander Chair of Excellence, for the first six months of my sabbatical (January to July 2010). In particular, I would like to thank President Juan José Romo Urroz and Dean Daniel Peña Sánchez de Rivera. They were not only instrumental in facilitating my integration into a new academic environment, they also provided me with the tools necessary to complete this work. I also owe a special debt of gratitude to professor José María Sauca Cano, who invited me to participate in the day-to-day activities of the Grupo de Investigaciones sobre el Derecho y la Justicia (GIDYD); this gesture is both indicative of José's intellectual generosity and the mark of an exceptional collegiality that I will not soon forget. I would also like to thank Professors Rafael Escudero, Carmen Pérez, Jesús Prieto de Pedro, Carlos Thiebaut, and Isabel Wences, dean of the Department of Political Science. My daily interactions with doctoral students and postdoctoral fellows, including Eloisa González Hidalgo, Macarena Iribarne Gonzalez, Pedro Garzon Lopez, and Luis G. Romero, helped me to better understand the similarities and differences among the Spanish, Mexican, and Canadian socio-political contexts. In all, I will always remember the warm welcome that I received at Carlos III.

The timing of my stay at Carlos III and, more specifically, at la Residencia de estudiantes du Consejo superior de investigaciones cientificas proved to be propitious for the writing of this book. It allowed me to witness first-hand a Spain in the grips of a spectrum of national and multinational emotions. In but six months, I saw Spain's diverse national consciousness swing from the lows brought on by a devastating economic crisis, increasing unemployment, a simmering constitutional crisis, and the lingering process of the Constitutional Tribunal to the unfettered explosion of patriotism stemming from the country's victory in the 2010 World Cup.

The ideas and arguments advanced in *Minority Nations in the Age of Uncertainty* draw their roots especially from my interactions with two major intellectual networks. On the Basque, Catalan, Galician, and Spanish side, I wish to thank Xavier Arbós Marín, Joxerramon Bengoetxea Caballero, Agusti Colomines i Companys, Francisco Colom González, André Fazi, Enric Fossas Espadaler, Montserrat Guibernau, Daniel Innerarity, Ramón Máiz Suárez, Luis Moreno Fernández, Ferran Requejo Coll, Carles Viver i Pi-Sunyer, and Eduardo J. Ruiz Vieytez. In Canada and Quebec, I would like to highlight the contributions of Jacques Beauchemin, James Bickerton, Stephen Brooks, Gérard Bouchard, Eugénie Brouillet, Linda Cardinal, Jan Erk, Bernard Gagnon, Raffaele Iacovino, Dimitrios Karmis, Guy Laforest, André Lecours, Jocelyn Maclure, John McGarry, Geneviève Nootens, the late Richard Simeon, François Rocher, Michel Seymour, A. Brian Tanguay, James Tully, Luc Turgeon, and José Woerhling. I would also like to point out the important off-stage help provided to me by the following individuals at different stages of the writing process: Olivier De Champlain, Xavier Dionne, Mathieu Huard-Champoux, Louiselle Lévesque, Daniel Pfeffer, Alexander Schwartz, and Marc Woons. I would like to express my gratitude to Arjun Tremblay of Concordia University in Montreal. His help in adapting and translating large segments of *L'âge des incertitudes* and in making the wording punchier and more direct was crucial to the successful completion of this project. Lastly, many thanks go to people at the University of Toronto Press, especially John St James and Daniel Quinlan, for their professionalism and continued support during the preparation of the English version of this work.

MINORITY NATIONS IN THE AGE OF UNCERTAINTY

New Paths to National Emancipation and Empowerment

Introduction: National Cultures, Democracy, and Legitimacy

Without a doubt, embracing multinationalism also requires accepting the principle of uncertainty; however, is not uncertainty at the heart of the democratic experience.

Alain Dieckhoff[1]

This book develops three major arguments. First, the survival of minority nations is tenuous despite an ostensible shift, in global politics, towards the politicization and enshrinement of diversity; minority nations now live in an age of uncertainty. Second, current approaches to the management of diversity and to national emancipation are limited in scope. On the one hand, an overreliance on the value of federal institutions obfuscates the persistence of homogenizing and undemocratic political practices and, ultimately, a tacit acceptance of the unattainability of the federal culture. On the other hand, national mobilization vested in a homogeneous conception of identity and fixed unilaterally on sovereignty discounts a priori the importance of intra-national cooperation and conciliation; minority nations must not overlook the communities living within their territories in their struggle for recognition lest they perpetuate the cycle of imperialism. Third, the survival of minority nations as democratic entities rests both on their empowerment vis-à-vis the central government and on their capacity to "empower" groups and communities living within their territory.

In this book, I approach the issue of minority nations using an essay style of writing. That said, herein I do not embark on a comprehensive empirical analysis, but instead aim to draw upon a variety of quantitative and normative works in order to provide a unique multidisciplinary approach towards the understanding of minority nations and the uncertainties that they face. Drawing upon the works of philosophers, political theorists, scholars of nationalism, and comparativists, among others, this book aims to provide cutting-edge analysis of how minority nations can ensure their continued place in today's world.

The last few centuries have witnessed the disappearance of the great empires and, concomitantly, the global eclosion of the nation state. Since the end of the Second World War, more than 110 new nation states have seen the light of day. Paradoxically, the number of nation states has more than tripled since the mid-twentieth century despite predictions that state formation is a thing of the past. On the heels of the disintegration of the Austro-Hungarian and Ottoman Empires and the retreat of European colonizers from North America and Latin America, the last century has also seen the retreat of colonial forces from Asia[2] and Africa.[3] This retreat has meant the birth of new countries and the development of a politics of hope for peoples still living under the yoke of the tutelary state. The dismantling of the Soviet Union has had a similar effect and, over the last twenty years, a slew of new independent states have emerged across Eastern Europe.

To be clear, in the absence of strong opposition movements and open rebellion, some empires tolerated the existence of minority nations or cultural groups within their often wide territorial expanse. However, this precarious arrangement hinged solely on minority groups acknowledging the uncontested power of emperors and their representatives. Within this context, it was possible for these groups to live according to their norms and traditions as long as they accepted the "legitimate" authority of the conqueror or colonizer. A prime institutional example of the arrangement between majority and minority nations is the Act of Quebec; its adoption in 1774 did little to reconcile deep national cleavages, but it ensured French Canadian loyalty to the British Crown.

Empires also tolerated the continued existence of cultural groups as long as forms of toleration did not challenge imperial or monarchical authority. This mode of conduct can help to explain why some empires – or, in the words of Louis Snyder,[4] "macro-national" entities – proved more resilient to change; they exchanged the toleration of diversity for minority acquiescence to their legitimate authority. In fact, the persistence of empires is perhaps better explained by this calculation than it is by processes of cultural homogenization. For example, Britain's colonial empire proved to be far more stable than its French counterpart; whereas the French institutionalized quasi-apartheid[5] forms of racial segregation, the English engaged local elites and strongmen as agents of the throne. In the latter case, this entailed a less than philanthropic acceptance of diversity that, nonetheless, buttressed the power of the colonial authority.

The nation state is now the most advanced and widely accepted political arrangement. However, its modern origins differ significantly. In the wake of the Second World War and, subsequently, the end of the Cold War, democratization led to the development of new nation states. In Africa and Asia, nation state–making was the outcome of decolonization. Decolonization has also inspired minority communities in North America and Western and Central Europe to articulate their own claims to nation statehood. This has been the case, inter alia, for the peoples of Quebec, Scotland, and Catalonia. The cross-national link between emancipatory projects is most readily highlighted in the works of Kenneth McRoberts, Michael Hechter, Montserrat Guibernau, and Michael Keating.[6]

Over the last few decades, "nations without states"[7] have sought greater recognition and political authority within modern democracies.[8] This new political project has been propelled by three interrelated factors. First, it has been driven by the desire, among constituents and elites of minority nations, to rupture with the past and to *make history*. Second, it is also motivated by the recognition and affirmation of communal values within minority nations that can and should be the constitutive components of a project intended *to make a society*.[9] Third, it has been propelled by an attempt to deepen democracy through nationalism rather than in opposition to it.

Given the crystallization of national identity in post-referenda Quebec, the forthcoming referendum on national sovereignty in Scotland, and the renewed national mobilization in Catalonia, we must ask whether these developments presage a new wave of nation-state formation. Each of these cases bear evidence that national majorities have yet to respond justly to national minority claims making. In Quebec, following the failure of the 1995 referendum on national sovereignty, the central state was quick to curtail other provincial policy initiatives.[10] In Spain, constitutional negotiations over Catalonia's autonomous status are now at an impasse. In fact, the Constitutional Tribunal's response to Catalan demands has undone much of the goodwill between Catalonia and the central state and has reaffirmed the latter's unilateral supremacy by imposing a new constitutional order. The Tribunal's decision displeased all political factions in Catalonia, save for those with ties to national populist parties. Catalans took to the streets as they did during Spain's transition to democracy and, in general, political parties and civil society were united in condemning a decision that brought into question the ideal of popular sovereignty upon which the principle of "autonomous status" rests.

The Tribunal's decision has also strained the relationship of trust between Catalans and their fellow Spanish citizens. It declares, in fact, that references to Catalonia as a nation or as a de facto national entity are without basis in Spanish law. Other dispositions, such as the protection of Catalan as the primary language of public administration and public media, have been annulled. As one specialist in international law states:

> Catalonia's capacity to administer justice within its own territory has been impeded by the Constitutional Court of Spain, which has cancelled many of the powers conferred on the Catalan Executive Council by the Statute. Furthermore, several clauses relating to the region's jurisdiction over economic matters have been declared unconstitutional as has its "legislative capability to establish and regulate taxes levied by local governments."[11]

Faced with increased unreceptiveness to their claims – whether it be in Catalonia or in Quebec – national minorities often have no other option but to mobilize around a political project that may eventually lead to independence and to the break-up of the nation state. Two recent films have brought to light the continued desire of national minorities to have their cultural, identitary, economic, institutional, and political aspirations recognized by the central state. Dolors Genoves's *Adeu, Espanya* focuses on Catalonia, Scotland, Greenland, and Quebec and Roger Boire and Jean-Pierre Roy's *Questions nationales* explores the possibility of successful Québécois, Catalan, and Scottish national mobilization.[12] Both of these films present themselves as forerunners of future developments if national majorities continue to be insensitive to and intransigent regarding legitimate minority claims making.[13]

Situating himself with the context of deeply divided societies, Miquel Caminal i Badia argues that political actors must demonstrate a new sense of maturity by renouncing dynamics of power and subjugation and by questioning the tacit acceptance of the nation state's homogenizing imperative. He contends, in *El federalismo pluralista: Del federalismo nacional al federalismo plurinacional*, that we must re-conceptualize federalism and abandon the traditional "American" model anchored in unifying and centralizing principles. A new way of conceptualizing federalism would lead to the creation of a society rooted in inter-communal confidence and do away with ideas of threat and constraint.[14] This new federalism would also entail the realization of a true "federal culture" by requiring the renegotiation of institutional arrangements between the state's founding nations. In advancing this new understanding of federalism, Caminal i Badia echoes Joseph Proudhon: "The idea of the federation is the apotheosis of political thought ... It resolves all the difficulties brought about by the pact between liberty and authority ... The opposition of these principles now appears to be the necessary conditions for a universal equilibrium."[15] The search for this balance is difficult to achieve; it is in fact an ideal that we should strive to realize. Majority nations have, in large part, overlooked this ideal in an attempt to master the political arena and, in turn, have created an environment marked by significant inter-national tensions and the mobilization of opposition groups.

We now find ourselves in a period of great uncertainty. All over the world, national minorities feel that national majorities are unreceptive to the most important of their national and identitary claims. However, nation states are focused almost exclusively on addressing non-identitary issues such as international economic competiveness and the impact of globalization; remedying the growing fiscal crisis; poverty and epidemics; transnational migration; terrorism; and unfettered energy consumption. While these issues are important and require the mobilization of political and economic resources, they should not be used as a pretext to avoid responding to the legitimate claims of national minorities within a plurinational context.

It is much too early to know for sure the outcome of the growing tension between majorities and national minorities given that political actors have a tendency to downplay or altogether ignore both the roots and salience of legitimate minority claims making. Several factors must be taken into account in order to determine the extent to which states will be able to maintain, deepen, or lose their legitimate authority over their constitutive national groups; these factors can be of a "differentialist," sociological, institutional, or ideological nature.[16] What we can say for sure is that as long as majority and minority nations are unable to communicate along the same wavelength, it is more than likely that inter-national tensions will increase.

The Spanish case is a prime example of this pattern. More than three decades after the transition to democracy and the recognition of the state's autonomous regions in 1978,[17] the country has not been able to fully implement its multinational model and, accordingly, satisfy the demands of the historical nations that have greatly contributed to its international distinctiveness and to the entrenchment of its fledgling democratic institutions. After having refused, in 2008, to recognize the Basque country's claim to national self-determination, the Constitutional Tribunal invalidated, on 28 June 2010, many of the new powers accorded to the Catalan government by the popular referendum on 18 June 2006.[18] These decisions undoubtedly suggest to members of both the Basque and Catalan nations that they may be better off pushing for national independence than continue negotiations with the central state.[19] Ironically, popular consultation in Catalonia was preceded by votes of support in both the national and sub-state parliaments. However, the Partido Popular (PP) was quick to push forward a constitutional motion that suspended the political pact between the Spanish and Catalan governments. In addition to the opposition coming from the PP, legal challenges came from the Ombudsman (Defensor del Pueblo) in tandem with five other autonomous regions, namely Aragon, Balearic Islands, Murcia, La Rioja, and the Valencian community.[20] It is hard to predict the real impact of this constitutional motion; nonetheless, it will be very difficult to recreate bonds of confidence between the central state, the government of Catalonia, and the members of the Catalan nation.

Within the context of such inter-national tensions, we can detect two distinct conceptualizations of the state. On the one hand, we find the "Jacobin vision" that values the centralizing power of the state and the will to integrate national minorities under the auspices of a singular national project without having recourse to the politics of accommodation. The French Revolution of 1789, driven by Jacobinism, was not content with simply liquidating the *ancien régime*; it sought to create a new ideology. As John Loughlin reminds us: "During the course of the nineteenth century, the nation-state led to the creation of a new political philosophy that was to rival the other ideologies of modernity, including socialism, liberalism, and reactionary conservatism; that philosophy was nationalism."[21] The Jacobin project advocated the entrenchment of an egalitarian society and sought to put an end to aristocratic privilege, and was ultimately unresponsive to any idea of recognizing deep difference within the state. On the other hand, the "Girondin vision" of the state values the importance of enshrining ethno-cultural difference as a constitutive component of the nation state. Nonetheless, by opposing universal suffrage and the abolition of slavery, the Girondin project sat squarely on the conservative end of the French ideological spectrum. In sum, "true" nationalists should be seen as advocates, in the Jacobin tradition, of a state solely for themselves, whereas national minorities are proponents of a federal utopia that has over the years been promoted by great thinkers such as Althusius, Proudhon, Montesquieu, and Pi i Margall.

The Jacobin tradition is strong and has a seductive appeal: it promises the enshrinement of social harmony and the creation of a single and indivisible nation through the subjugation or elimination of socio-political sources of opposition. Jacobinism is averse to any form of disagreement, be it reasonable or not. Modern democratic societies must emancipate themselves from this ideology in order to make way for the development of a socio-political environment that enshrines a true sense of freedom and that allows for national self-determination. It is, however, difficult to conceptualize a new reality in which each nation has its own state. There are more than ten thousand diverse cultures that are now claiming some form of recognition or autonomy. Furthermore, due to the large number of nations in the modern world, it is also difficult to envisage nation-state formation as the only means of satisfying identitary claims. However, these factors should not lead us to dismiss a priori claims for national sovereignty. In fact, over the last half-century, the international community has accepted, concomitantly, a certain degree of political instability and has accommodated the development of more than 100 new nation states. As James Tully noted in 1995: "The international system would still be workable if, say, East Timor separated from Indonesia, Scotland from United Kingdom, Catalonia from Spain, Quebec from Canada or the predominantly Spanish-speaking states from the United States."[22]

Anthony Smith reminds us that fewer than 10 per cent of ethno-cultural nations have their own state.[23] It thus behoves us to imagine ways in which we can accommodate diversity and distinct national identities so that communities can live together under the auspices of peace and harmony.[24] Having stated this, however, we should not accept that the national majority establish, in and of itself, the criteria by which a national minority can rely upon popular sovereignty as the basis for actualizing self-determination. The Supreme Court of Canada's reference on the secession of Quebec provides some insight into how an equitable process of national self-determination could play out:

> However, we are equally unable to accept the reverse proposition, that a clear expression of self-determination by the people of Quebec would impose no obligations upon the other provinces or the federal government. The continued existence and operation of the Canadian constitutional order cannot remain indifferent to the clear expression of a clear majority of Quebecers that they no longer wish to remain in Canada. This would amount to the assertion that other constitutionally recognized principles necessarily trump the clearly expressed democratic will of the people of Quebec. Such a proposition fails to give sufficient weight to the underlying constitutional principles that must inform the amendment process, including the principles of democracy and federalism. The rights of other provinces and the federal government cannot deny the right of the government of Quebec to pursue secession, should a clear majority of the people of Quebec choose that goal, so long as in doing so, Quebec respects the rights of others. Negotiations would be necessary to address the interests of the federal government, of Quebec and the other provinces, and other participants, as well as the rights of all Canadians both within and outside Quebec.[25] (paragraph 92)[26]

It is important to return, at this point, to one of the main questions driving contemporary research on national minorities: is the onset of a new wave of nation-state-making inevitable? As we will see in chapter 5, existing nation states have thus far been reticent to accept new entrants into the fraternity of nation states. This reticence or resistance is perhaps most noticeable in Canada and Spain. Spain, at the end of the first decade of the twenty-first century, is reminiscent of Canada's two post-referenda periods (the years following the 1980 and 1995 referenda on national sovereignty). Mounting evidence suggests that there is little, if any, possibility of enshrining asymmetrical federalism in either country. In fact, works by Hector Bofill (*Democràcia Cuirassada*)[27] and Daniel Turp (*La nation bâillonnée*)[28] point to growing democratic deficit in Canada and Spain and, concomitantly, to the hardening of the national majority's stance towards, respectively, national minority claims making in Catalonia and Quebec.

In the pages that follow, I examine how national minorities can and must advance their claims in an increasingly inhospitable environment and, in doing so, build on the rich literature on Québécois, Catalan, and Scottish national minorities.[29] This literature demonstrates that these nations, in spite of varying degrees of constraints, have been able to engage in effective self-governance. This book seeks to build on this work and to contribute a new approach to ideas of national self-determination and inter-national reconciliation. More specifically, I will argue that the next wave of nation-state formation cannot depend on the decline of empires and transnational imperialism. Rather, it will depend on the willingness of existing nation states to accommodate national diversity within their territorial boundaries. Catalonia, Scotland, and Quebec may well indeed be the vanguard of this new wave of nation-state formation if national majorities in Spain, the United Kingdom, and Canada fail to recognize and empower national minorities.

To be clear, national majorities have taken some steps to accommodate national minorities. Spain is no longer an autocratic polity; in the wake of the Franco regime, the central government demonstrated a certain degree of receptiveness to identitary claims making by establishing the system of autonomies. However, this formula must be revisited in light of the new demands for self-determination emanating from Basque and Catalan communities in particular. Since the mid-1960s, Canada has exhibited some degree of openness to Québécois claims making marked noticeably by Joe Clark's use of "community of communities" as a descriptor of the Canadian polis, by the rhetoric of the "distinct society" during the Mulroney years (1984–93), and, more recently, by the promulgation of "open federalism" during Stephen Harper's first two years in power (2006–8).[30] However, here too, the central government has been strongly resistant to the prospect of Québécois national self-determination.

Despite the impediments to the emergence of new nation states, we can nonetheless foresee the onset of a new wave of nation-state formation. This new wave is almost unstoppable given the emancipatory path laid out by preceding waves of nation-state formation. Within this context, a new wave of nationalism can provide a "structure of integration" allowing for the development of cross-polity solidarity and also providing the necessary resources for effective social integration and active citizenship.[31] The new wave of new nation states, in so far as it constitutes the creation of "integration structures" that are both open and plural, is of the utmost importance, as it will allow not only for the fulfilment of national determination but also for the channelling of collective identities into the interrelated projects of democratization and global justice.

Although the military-industrial-cultural complex is an important force in the modern world, it is hard if not impossible to imagine a return to older forms of imperialism. It is also impossible to imagine that nations and the idea of nationality can persist, in and of themselves, ad infinitum. Such a situation would complexify global governance beyond the scope of effectiveness and would also endanger the most at-risk national communities. Here multinational federalism provides a concrete option to the reconciliation of diversity and to the accommodation of national distinctiveness. This novel approach requires, however, that national communities undertake the reconstruction of the political sphere from the bottom up.

According to the multinational model, there is no need for founding nations to abandon their communal authority or their language. However, the transition to this new model of federalism within the context of modern democracy faces several challenges. As Marc Chevrier states: "Historically empires have been more accepting of the presence of a multitude of nations within their territories than have been nation-states. One need only think of the Austro-Hungarian Empire and the United Kingdom, which has never really become a nation-state."[32] Furthermore, the enshrinement of multinational federalism depends on the existence of a deep "federal culture" (see chapter 6) and on the national majority's ability to see this new model as both an instrument of stability as well as a mechanism for increasing its prestige and power at the global level. The majority nation must therefore be confident in its capacity to reproduce its customs/traditions/language over time. Switzerland[33] is an example of a "multicultural federation" (or, according to Will Kymlicka, a "multinational federation")[34] that has been able to accommodate diversity under the auspices of mutual respect between minority and majority groups.[35] The success of this political project is the result of the concomitant development of a high level of loyalty to common public institutions and to the promotion of adherence to institutions contained within the territory occupied by each linguistic community. In Canada and Spain, the situation is quite different: political elites are hesitant or outright reluctant to propose constitutional reforms that resonate with the demands of their respective state's founding nations and, in turn, this demonstrates that the political cultures of these countries are fragile and inherently insecure.

. This book provides six interrelated sketches on national minorities, on processes of accommodation, and on autonomy and self-determination within a modern democratic context. In chapter 1,

I explore the management of linguistic diversity in plurinational states and within the context of national models that give primacy to either communitarian or individual rights. Here, I focus on the evolution of language policy in Canada from a comparative perspective. In the Canadian context, political actors and dominant social groups have tended to advocate the entrenchment of individual rights, which, in turn, has traditionally served the purpose of maintaining power and authority over minority groups. Canada still has a long way to go to match the extent and depth of Switzerland's politics of linguistic accommodation. This has been brought to light in a recent report released by the Office of the Commissioner of Official Languages that condemns the federal government's laissez-faire approach to the promotion of French within the public sector.[36]

In chapter 2, I examine two of the major challenges to the persistence of national minorities: globalization and the entrenchment of overlapping citizenship regimes. Here, I focus on the Francophonie writ large in order to highlight the deleterious impact of American cultural imperialism and Anglo-homogenization on minority communities. No country is inured to these developments as evidenced by the adoption of policy countermeasures in European Union countries that aim to preserve cultural and linguistic distinctiveness.[37] Likewise, Anglo-homogenization has brought about an age of institutional conformity both at the inter-state and international levels that presents a significant challenge to the persistence of national minorities. I end this chapter with a brief discussion on the type of citizenship regime that is needed to counterbalance these forces and that can allow both for the maintenance of minority cultures and the redressing of social exclusion.

In chapter 3, I outline two novel ways of accommodating national minorities in their quest for formal recognition and autonomy: the affirmation of informal constitutions and the enshrinement of interculturalism. The first challenge that all national minorities face is that of breaking down the barriers that threaten to impoverish the developing political culture of a people engaged in nation building. This fledgling political culture may only survive and thrive if the leaders of the minority nation are capable of ensuring the recognition of a set of organic laws that serve as identitary, social, and political markers for the nation's citizenry. The second challenge derives from the need of all democratic polities to promote active citizen engagement, political participation, and public contestation. In both Catalonia and Quebec, the promulgation of active citizenship and the formalization of interculturalism have, in recent years, been inextricably linked. The intercultural model for managing diversity rejects the notion of juxtaposing groups (as opposed to the multicultural model) and instead encourages cross-cultural dialogue and the responsible re-founding of the political community.

In chapter 4, I invoke the works of political philosophers – in particular, Isaiah Berlin, Philip Pettit, and James Tully – in order to evaluate the tensions that exist between governmental policies that seek to contain so-called autonomous regions and those that attempt to empower these same regions. I will also explore the potential of two forms of self-determination (internal and external) as means for managing intercommunal conflicts. Within this context, I will argue that autonomy need not be seen as closing oneself off to the "Other"; rather, autonomy can and should be viewed as a mechanism of enfranchisement that is both voluntary and consensual. Finally, in this chapter I will explain why a politics of recognition is a necessary condition for the deepening of democracy, though also insufficient, in and of itself, to ensure its expansion and persistence over time.

In chapter 5, I evaluate the different ways in which the terms "community," "autonomy," and "empowerment" are operationalized in countries marked by deep diversity. Within this context, multinational federalism is presented as a promising model for managing sub-state national diversity. However, its adoption or formalization requires that states which can be described as multinational recognize that they do in fact constitute more than a single nation. Representatives of national minorities in democratic polities have employed other strategies in an attempt to create conditions for collaboration that are just to all relevant groups. For some time, and faced with the success of "indigenous" groups vis-à-vis international institutions, members of minority nations (e.g., Tatars, Chechens, Tibetans, Romani, and Palestinians)[38] have come to define themselves as the first inhabitants of a country and not as part of a larger community of nations. Concomitantly, plurinational nation states have hardened their stances vis-à-vis minority national, identitary, and collective claims making. In turn, this has been an impediment to inter-communal reconciliation. This situation requires that political and social actors as well as social scientists take immediate action to develop a bold strategic plan in order to reverse the current trend that is ultimately a gateway to cultural, social, and political homogenization.

In chapter 6, I re-conceptualize inter-communal reconciliation and the management of inter-ethnic conflict by invoking practices inherited from the past. Challenges to the persistence of minority nations within modern states bring us to rethink inter-communal relations and to draw inspiration from ancestral practices. I contend that the recent work on federalism and citizenship regimes has made it possible to re-conceptualize the basis of the political contract linking the constitutive nations of a complex democracy. Although this new approach is primarily normative, it nonetheless has real impact on the way in which inter-communal relations are both perceived and legitimized. In developing this approach, I begin by examining "pactism" and evaluating its normative contributions to contemporary society. Then I flesh out the idea of a "federal culture" as a necessary condition for the advent of a complex polity united by the belief in a shared future and imbued with an ethic of reciprocity. Finally, I examine a variant of federalism, "federalism by treaty," as a mechanism for managing diversity. I will argue that this type of federalism is the most suitable for responding to the demands of pactism and to the values underlying the implementation of a federal culture.

The right to govern is not inherited from the past. Rather, it is earned in the here and now; or to paraphrase Ernest Renan, political life must be a daily plebiscite. When we gaze through this aperture, we can contend that the advent and development of the nation state may once have represented the highest form of democracy since the onset of modernity, but that its persistence as a model of power and rule does not bestow existing nation states with incontestable legitimate authority over the fate of nations on the path to statehood. Thus, where the respect of minority rights is guaranteed, where democratic practices are deeply entrenched, where constitutionalism and the rule of law are respected, and where an ethos of solidarity is being developed, it is conceivable that new states can emerge in so far as they possess the necessary human and economic capital to ensure the emancipation of their communities.

Finally, in conclusion, I will provide the outlines for the development of a new politics based on the principles of moderation, dignity, and hospitality. This will allow us to conceptualize the management of national diversity based on principles that no self-respecting nation state can overlook and that must be fully enshrined in any and every contemporary nation state.

1 Linguistic Diversity, Language Policy, and the Limits of Federal Accommodation[1]

While the state can be neutral in regard to religion for example, it must use (a) language(s) to communicate with its citizenry. In choosing a language, or even multiple languages, the state exhibits a linguistic bias, most often that of the linguistic majority or dominant groups.

Selma K. Sonntag[2]

Federalism is a multifaceted tool: it is a mechanism for managing conflict, an instrument that helps mediate conflicting political agendas, and a shield meant to protect the rights and identities of territorial and non-territorial minorities. One of federalism's primary objectives is to balance the demands and interests of political units that are both sovereign and integrated in such a way that no unit or political community is left out of the policymaking process and that the national majority is prevented from unilaterally imposing its will on minority populations; accordingly, federalism allows for the evolution of distinct territorial majorities and, concomitantly, for the development of deep national diversity. Within this context, language policy is one of the main manifestations of the link between federalism and the persistence of difference.

This chapter focuses on the adoption and development of language policy within the Canadian federation and within the context of a foundational tension that has been both a source of the country's great diversity and a threat to the persistence of the Canadian polis over time. Canadian federalism, as we are reminded by the Supreme Court of Canada's ruling on Quebec's right to secession (1998), rests on four pillars: (1) democracy; (2) federalism; (3) constitutionalism and the rule of law; and (4) the protection of minority rights. Paradoxically, these pillars, which are ostensibly of equal normative value, create the appearance of a means through which collective emancipation can be realized, yet they also constitute the fundamental sources of tension between political actors in Canada.

Canada's language policies can help to shed new light on the tensions pervading other countries marked by deep national diversity. From the 1960s onwards, linguistic communities across the country have been increasingly vocal about the state's duty to recognize and accommodate minority languages. The origins of modern language politics can be traced back to Quebec's Quiet Revolution.[3] At the onset of the second half of the twentieth century, members of Quebec's francophone majority were second-class citizens.[4] For example, in 1961 French-speaking Québécois earned an average annual salary of $3185, whereas English Canadians earned an annual average salary of $3469. At the provincial level, the average French Québécois salary was 8 per cent lower than the province's cumulative average salary and 35 per cent lower than the average salary of an Anglo Quebecer (of British descent).[5] The growing friction between the disenfranchised francophone majority and the anglophone elite drove the central government to adopt a novel set of language policies. This history has had two interrelated effects in Quebec: it has made political actors more conscious of their responsibilities towards the protection of the French language and it has incited the Québécois state to develop a plan of action that links language policy with a larger emancipatory project that also comprises the entrenchment of cultural, economic, institutional, political, and social justice.

In this chapter, I focus on three aspects of language policy. First, I highlight the differences between two types of bilingual federal arrangements: one that is based on the principle of "territoriality" and the other that is of a "personal" nature. Second, I examine the origins and development of language policy and linguistic accommodation in Canada. This examination will bring to light the dynamic of "pressure" and "attraction" that is at the heart of Canada's language debate. Third, I expand the analytical aperture to focus on three other cases of linguistic accommodation in federal polities: New Brunswick, Nunavut, and Catalonia. In brief, I contend that the emphasis on a "personal" conception of bilingualism is a threat to the persistence of the French language in Canada, that federal language policy promotes the "attractiveness" of English and does little to alleviate the "pressure" on the survival of French, that the problems confronting national minorities in Canada are not uncommon, and, more important, that federalism itself is not a sufficient condition to ensure that minority languages and cultures survive and thrive over time.

"Personal," "Territorial," and "Institutional" Bilingualism

Canada is a country in which several regimes of language rights coexist. These rights have often been invoked in constitutional clauses. Examples include section 133 of the British North America Act (BNA) 1867, section 19 of the Canadian Charter of Rights and Freedoms 1982 (which confirmed the validity of applying section 133 to federal institutions and extended its scope to include the province of New Brunswick), and section of 23 of the Manitoba Act 1870. Furthermore, across Canada, individuals can use either of the two official languages in courts falling under the jurisdiction of the central government.

The existence of a federal system in Canada has meant that demands for language rights have been filtered through institutions in different ways and that they have led to different results. These demands have also varied from one province to another depending on their moment of entry into the confederation. Within this context, New Brunswick is the province where linguistic rights are the most formally recognized due to their later enshrinement in the constitution; however, it should be noted that this has yet to translate into a more equitable treatment of the province's francophone and anglophone constituencies.

Three major approaches have been privileged for taking into account the variety of options under which language regimes have mobilized and advanced their claims: (1) unilingualism; (2) personal bilingualism; (3) territorial bilingualism.

Major tensions have flared up, albeit sporadically, between proponents of unlingualism (such as the Confederation of Regions [CoR] political party in New Brunswick), personal bilingualism (Canada outside of Quebec), and territorial bilingualism (Quebec). Nonetheless, since the mid-1960s, federal politicians have promoted the entrenchment of "institutional bilingualism," a model for managing linguistic diversity that Canadians have been generally inclined to favour.

Theoretical contributions by comparative political scientists, in particular Kenneth D. McRae and Jean Laponce, are of particular importance in helping to further distinguish the aforementioned types of bilingualism. On the one hand, personal bilingualism refers to the rights that an individual may or may not call upon to employ wherever

Table 1 Knowledge of an official language, by province and territory

	Total	English only	French only	French and English	Neither French nor English
Canada	31,241,030	21,129,945	4,141,850	5,448,850	520,380
Quebec	7,435,905	336,785	4,010,880	3,017,860	70,375
Ontario	12,028,895	10,335,705	49,210	1,377,325	266,660
Atlantic	2,257,555	1,803,710	74,900	375,870	3,055
West	5,343,715	4,911,020	4,615	373,855	54,230
British Columbia	4,074,385	3,653,365	2,070	295,645	123,305
Territories	100,575	89,355	175	8,275	2,760

Source: Statistics Canada, 2006 Census of Population.

Table 2 Knowledge of both French and English in 1951, 1971, and 2001 (% of population)

	1951	1971	2001
Canada	12.1	13.4	17.7
Quebec	25.8	27.6	40.8
Canada outside of Quebec	6.9	8.0	10.3

Source: Louise Marmen and Jean-Pierre Corbeil, *Languages in Canada. 2001 Census*, New Canadian Perspectives Series (Ottawa: Canadian Heritage and Statistics Canada, 2004), 154–8.

he or she decides to reside. In this case, it befalls the individual to choose in which language he or she will receive government services. On the other hand, territorial bilingualism posits that rights are linked to the place where an individual resides. That is to say that under the auspices of a "territorial" model, minorities must adjust to the majority's linguistic preferences within a given territory.[6] In the context of a multinational federation, an individual might expect that dominant language patterns would reflect certain demographic realities. However, for a number of reasons, personal bilingualism is not fully applicable in Canada, whereas territorial bilingualism has yet to be fully implemented due to the central government's role in the design and management of languages policies.

This choice of models is not without consequence; it reveals a particular vision of the country that, in turn, is rooted in distinct conceptualizations of federalism. Personal bilingualism invites individuals to express their preferences through the use of their primary language (i.e., their mother tongue) when interacting with federal institutions, whereas territorial bilingualism establishes clear linguistic boundaries within which individuals interact with institutions; the concomitant promotion of these different models is meant to engender social cohesion. It is interesting to note, however, that the members of the Royal Commission on Bilingualism and Biculturalism seemed to favour a territorial approach to managing linguistic diversity. The commission's 1965 preliminary report reads: "The chief protagonists, whether they are entirely conscious of it or not, are French-speaking Quebec and English-speaking Canada. And it seems to us to be no longer the traditional conflict between a majority and a minority. It is rather a conflict between two majorities: that which is a majority in all Canada, and that which is a majority in the entity of Quebec."[7]

Canada's language regime is a hybrid of personal and territorial models of bilingualism; in other words, the Canadian model for managing linguistic diversity is a form of "institutional bilingualism." With the adoption of the Official Languages Act in 1969, the federal government attempted to enshrine a dual system of languages rights that would transcend provincial divisions and reify its jurisdiction over this policy domain. In doing so, the federal government launched a series of initiatives meant to affirm the rights of linguistic minorities across the country (i.e., anglophones in Quebec and francophones in the rest of Canada). The entrenchment of language rights in the Canadian Charter of Rights and Freedoms in 1982 is a clear affirmation of this particular approach to managing linguistic diversity.

The federal government's initiatives also had important repercussions in Quebec where allophones (non-francophone and non-anglophone) invariably asked to be served in English when dealing with municipal and provincial public institution; these demands were antithetical to the spirit of the Charter of the French Language (often referred to as Bill 101 or, in French, la Charte de la langue française), which had made French the official language of Quebec. Still today, anglophone businesses with fifty or more employees must communicate with the Quebec state in French.[8] Nonetheless, even though the Charte de la langue française was adopted by the Quebec government over thirty-five years ago, Quebec's political institutions continue to provide services in English. This practice is most noticeable in Revenu Québec, Investissement Québec, and l'Autorité des marchés financiers, as well as several other agencies and governmental organizations. In turn, this demonstrates that the Quebec state has yet to fully embrace its duty to promote the French language. A similar pattern is evidenced at the municipal level: Montreal, the most significant French city in North America, does not hesitate to offer services in both languages. When these phenomena are noted, one can argue that institutional bilingualism is the norm in Quebec. Despite the fact that constituents in Quebec have demonstrated a strong preference for the enshrinement of territorial bilingualism, the persistent use of English in public institutions signals that the latter have a tendency to operate in opposition to provincial law.[9] Moreover, by facilitating the continued use of English in their dealings with allophones, Quebec's public institutions favour the development of a form of institutional bilingualism that leans clearly towards the "personal" rather than the "territorial" end of the spectrum. This type of institutional bilingualism is contributing to the erosion of linguistic diversity in Canada and, in turn, evidences a gap between the promulgation of language policies de jure and their de facto application.

In sum, Quebec's role as the main pillar of Canada's language regime is tentative at best. In the following section, I will argue that this role is further threatened by a process of "pressure" and "attraction" within the polity's political institutions, which, for the most part, are biased towards the protection and promotion of English in North America. Within this context, the tension between linguistic groups has a real impact on the use and protection of languages themselves. For example, the power of attraction of the English language is such that it privileges the development of a weak policy of linguistic protection for a minority language. Given the efforts needed to counteract the growth of the majority language, this dynamic also entails the weakening of public policies that seek to ensure the formal equality of English and French.

Language Regimes: The "Push and Pull" Dynamic

It is very rare to find a situation where linguistic groups are treated equally or are given the same opportunities to flourish economically and socially. Canada is no exception to this general pattern. However, what is truly surprising in the Canadian case is the amount of time that it took for the federal government to adopt some form of corrective public policy intended to redress the disenfranchisement of the country's francophone minority. The Quebec government's promulgation of Bill 63 (Loi pour promouvoir la langue française au Québec) in 1969 signalled the advent of a "push and pull" dynamic that has since marked the relationship between the federal government and the Quebec state as it relates to language policy.[10]

The tensions between linguistic groups in Canada led the federal government to establish, in 1963, the Royal Commission on Bilingualism and Biculturalism (a.k.a. the Laurendeau-Dunton commission). The commission's report revealed that, for a variety of reasons, French Canadians had been victims of a systemic pattern of discrimination and occupied a lower rung on the socio-economic ladder.[11] The report also revealed that French Canadians were not only underrepresented in public sector and the military but also, when present in these institutions, had a greater tendency to occupy subordinate positions.[12]

The Laurendeau-Dunton commission examined four countries where some form of official bilingualism had been adopted: Belgium, Finland, Switzerland, and South Africa. The South African case, where a large portion of the population had access to Afrikaans and English language facilities, was of particular interest to the commission. In this context, the personal approach to bilingualism dominated; a South African could receive public services in either language irrespective of which part of the country he or she was living in. On the flip side, a territorial approach to bilingualism was more evident in Belgium and Switzerland, where one could observe a certain degree of overlap between territorial boundaries and the distribution of linguistic groups; the official language of the majority group within a specific territory determined the language that was used in public institutions, with the notable exception of Brussels (city and region), where citizens could demand services in either of two languages (Dutch or French). Finally, the commission argued that the Finnish model, which designated language districts (or local governmental units) according to a "10 per cent rule" (and a minimum of 5000 inhabitants), constituted the optimal mode for managing linguistic diversity.

Faced with important changes to the composition of its society, the Quebec state initiated its own discussion on language regimes in the mid-1960s. In the beginning, culture (more so than the economy, which at the time was controlled by the Anglo-Canadian bourgeoisie)[13] was seen as the primary arena for political action in spite of the dearth of initiatives undertaken to redress the disenfranchisement of francophones both in Quebec and in the rest of Canada. In response to the Laurendeau-Dunton commission's investigation, the Quebec government decided to establish its own investigatory commission – la Commission d'enquête sur la situation de la langue française et des droits linguistiques au Québec (Commission Gendron) – in order to identify the array of options available to the state of Quebec relating to the protection and promotion of the French language. The commission's launch was at a moment of significant upheaval in the province which involved a societal push for the articulation and affirmation of francophone identity and the state's transformation into the primary actor for national assertion and into the spokesperson for the emancipation of French Canadians in Quebec.[14]

However, the "pull" of the English language, in particular its appeal to immigrant groups as the ostensible means to ensure socio-economic mobility and prestige, proved to be an impediment to the realization of the ambitions of French Québécois. In the beginning, immigrants did not constitute a viable linguistic threat, given that very few opted to settle in Quebec. Nonetheless, with the gradual erosion of international borders, more and more immigrants have come to settle in Quebec.[15] Within this context, the city of Montreal has been profoundly reshaped by recent waves of immigration.[16] A large number of Montreal's immigrant communities adopted English as their language of primary usage and this has forestalled their integration into Quebec's social and political networks. Table 3, below, highlights the strong "pull" of the English language for new immigrants, but it also points to the efficiency of public policies implemented by the Quebec government meant to ensure the entrenchment of French as the province's common public language; this approach was adopted principally as a means to assert the facticity of French and to secure the economic emancipation of francophones. However, this approach also contributed to the deepening of social cohesion, the promotion of active citizenship, and the implementation of an intercultural approach to managing diversity that has a promising future (see chapter 3).

The federal government's most impactful decision was the adoption of official bilingualism in 1969. Seeking to counteract the prevailing tendency, the new policy sought to "ensure respect for English and French as the official languages of Canada and ensure equality of status and equal rights and privileges as to their use in all federal institutions, in particular with respect to their use in parliamentary proceedings, in legislative and other instruments, in the administration of justice, in

Table 3 Language shifts towards French and English among allophones (1971–2006)

Language shift	1971	1996	2001	2006
Towards French	29%	39%	46%	51%
Towards English	71%	61%	54%	49%

Source: Louise Marmen and Jean-Pierre Corbeil, *Nouvelles perspectives canadiennes. Les langues au Canada*, Recensement 2001, Ministère des Travaux publics et Services gouvernementaux, 2004; Statistics Canada, Recensement 2006: 97–555-XIF.

communicating with or providing services to the public and in carrying out the work of federal institutions."[17] The new policy also sought, albeit indirectly, to reify the federal government's authority over immigrants and immigration and also placed the polity's two principal languages on equal legal footing. Paradoxically, the language policy did little to counteract the "pull" of the English language and, ironically, reasserted the de facto subordinate role of French in the Canadian context.

Nevertheless, the Liberal governments of Pierre Elliott Trudeau undertook steps to remedy the numerical underrepresentation of francophones in the federal public sector. The Official Languages Act helped to increase francophone representation, over six decades, from 12.25 per cent in 1946 (when francophones accounted for 30 per cent of the Canadian population) to 27 per cent in 2004 (when the francophone population had decreased dramatically to 23 per cent of the Canadian constituency).[18] In 1978, only 14 per cent of all public sector jobs required functional bilingualism; the number increased to 38 per cent by 2005. Most (78%) of these positions have been filled by francophones, with a strong overrepresentation of francophones with a province of origin other than Quebec.[19]

Among its primary recommendations, the Laurendeau-Dunton commission proposed the creation of bilingual districts capable of providing, where possible, services in English and French in governmental agencies and offices. This recommendation was overlooked for a number of reasons, the primary one being that other provinces were vocally opposed to its implementation.[20]

Following the failure of this initiative, groups of non-francophones and non-anglophones began to mobilize and demanded that their opinions be taken into account in the design of new political arrangements. This "third force," as it was called at the time, exercised so strong an influence on federal policymakers in Ottawa that these politicians eventually decided to abandon the idea of biculturalism and instead opted to promulgate a *policy of multiculturalism* starting in 1971. This new policy could also be seen as the instrumentalization of ethnocultural minority claims making and the embodiment of two different conceptualizations of diversity: multiculturalism and multinationalism.[21] It also engendered a vocal reply from the Quebec state and a heretofore unseen mobilization of French Québécois.[22]

Multicultural public policy is still in place and was constitutionally enshrined under section 27 of the Constitution Act 1982, which states that "this Charter shall be interpreted in a manner consistent with the preservation and enhancement of the multicultural heritage of Canadians." In sum, all sections of the Charter must be compatible with section 27.

On the other hand, the Gendron commission's recommendations invited the Quebec state to play a more active role in the design and implementation of language policy. With the release of the commission's report, one could sense the Quebec government's desire to assert its leadership in an attempt to encourage immigrants to choose French instead of English as a language of instruction, as a language of commerce, and as a language of quotidian communication; in other words, as the language of the public sphere.

Following the release of the commission's report, the Bourassa government opted to make French the province's official language by adopting Bill 22. However, Bill 22 elicited more opposition than it did praise. For francophones, the bill was seen as a weak attempt at linguistic preservation, whereas anglophones denounced the coercive nature of the bill and refused to acknowledge the Quebec state's jurisdiction over language policy. In turn, the Quebec Liberal government lost much of its support from the Anglo community and lost the 1976 elections. Ironically, the Anglo backlash opened the door for an independentist faction to seize the reins of power under the charismatic leadership of René Lévesque[23] who sought to establish an equitable relationship between Quebec and the rest of Canada.

Following the Parti Québécois's victory in 1976 and the adoption of la Charte de la langue française in 1977, the state implemented the Program d'enseignement des langues d'origine in 1978. This program was designed to facilitate the integration of allophone children into their host society and also offered classes for these children to learn the languages spoken at home by their parents and grandparents. By allowing children of newcomers to learn the languages of their country of origin, the program sought to both encourage young people to learn the language of their host society and to maintain their cultural heritage.[24]

The implementation of a policy of official unilingualism was not without its critics; the federal government and Québécois anglophones were determined to defend the cross-polity model of institutional bilingualism. This defence manifested itself in the form of a series of judicial challenges that attempted to overturn or weaken "Bill 101," as the Charte de la langue française is commonly termed.[25] The latter, seen as an intensification of certain aspects of Bill 22, went further in identifying and establishing new avenues for the promotion of the French language (i.e., schools, workplace, billboards, etc.). Many anglophones and allophones left Quebec following the adoption of Bill 101.[26] Immigrants were sometimes of the opinion that although they were required to learn English as a condition for their integration into Canadian society, it was unjust to exempt long-established minorities (Québécois and Indigenous peoples) from learning the language of the majority. According to these same immigrants, if the acquisition of English could be generalized Canada would undoubtedly become an ideal place to live in the absence of linguistic disharmony. However, this argument is inapplicable in a federal context based on a multinational pact (see chapter 6).[27]

Three Case Studies

Canada's experience with the management of linguistic diversity can shed new light on other polities marked by sociological multilingualism. Linguistic mobilization in Quebec, within the broader context of a multinational federation, helped to force the linguistic majority to tolerate the institutionalization of language rights. As a result, several Canadian institutions, such as the army, the public service, and political institutions have gradually opened themselves up to francophones.

Following the unilateral patriation of the Constitution in 1981–2, Canada's federal government provided financial assistance to minority language groups (anglophones in Quebec and francophone communities in Canada outside Quebec) by launching the Court Challenges Program (CCP) with a mission to finance court cases and other forms of legal action intended to help implement the language rights guaranteed (but inadequately defined) by the Constitution Act, 1982. This program contributed to the development of an important form of jurisprudence which was used by minority language groups in Quebec and elsewhere in Canada. It also contributed, albeit to varying degrees, to the entrenchment of both institutional and personal forms of bilingualism.

With the enshrinement of the Canadian Charter of Rights and Freedoms in 1982, the status of the English and French languages acquired a certain degree of importance through judicial interpretation. Through this process, the federal government took on a more important role in the realm of language policy. This change was viewed with suspicion in certain parts of the country and, in particular, in Quebec, where the French language was at risk of being "pushed" to the margins as a result of immigration, a decrease in the francophone birth rate, and the "pull" of English as the language of social mobility. It was no surprise therefore that francophone opposition to the CCP was strongest in Quebec and that francophones living in other parts of Canada were largely supportive of this new legislation.

Québécois continue to perceive Canada as a country made up of two host societies, each capable of integrating newcomers and of offering them equal opportunity to maximize their life chances. The Quebec state has acquired, following the PQ's election in 1976 and through a series of political initiatives (such as the policy agendas of political parties, constitutional proposals, private member bills, etc.), considerable control over immigration. In turn, many of these initiatives have helped to attenuate certain tensions within the Canadian federation. The Quebec state has been able to assume a certain degree of control over the selection of newcomers, whereas Ottawa has retained control over the process of family reunification and the selection of refugees. In an attempt to promote social cohesion within its own society, the Quebec state has implemented a concerted yet imprecise policy of interculturalism that pushes immigrants to adopt the French language, to participate actively in society, to uphold democratic values, and to embrace a pluralist perspective that is sensitive to the protection of political and social rights.

The success of francophones in achieving some of their objectives has had an immediate impact on other national groups, for example: (1) within Canada (such as Acadians in New Brunswick and the Innus in Nunavut), (2) in other federal states (such as the Flemish in Belgium), and (3) in states undergoing a process of federalization (such as the autonomous communities in Spain). The cases of Nunavut and Catalonia are good examples of the implementation of a framework for the empowerment of linguistic minorities. Three cases will be addressed briefly in the pages that follow: New Brunswick, Nunavut, and Catalonia.

New Brunswick

In 1969, the government of New Brunswick adopted the first iteration of its Official Languages Act. Today, all provinces and territories – with the exception of British Columbia and Newfoundland – have laws in place that recognize both official languages and that allow for the provision of services in French.[28] New Brunswick's Official Languages Act 2002 guarantees that any individual in the province can receive services from public institutions in the language of his or her choice. Over the years, the government of New Brunswick has attempted to accommodate and help francophones living in the northern part of the province by adopting a series of remedial policies and through the implementation of laws such as the Act Recognizing the Equality of the Two Official Linguistic Communities in New Brunswick (1981), the Education Act (1997) and the Official Languages Act (1988, revised in 2004).

These policies have helped to contain the assimilation of the province's francophone population who, since 1931, have in increasing numbers attested in censuses to their French roots, but have declared English as their spoken language.[29] One thing is clear, New Brunswick's language policies have, at the bare minimum, helped to maintain the proportion of francophones in the province: in 1971, 33.8 per cent of the population was classified as francophone and in 2006, the francophone proportion of the population hovered around 32.8 per cent.[30] The effectiveness of the province's language policies is also evidenced by the Francophone population's low transfer rate towards the English language. To be sure, between 2001 and 2006, the transfer rate increased from 9.7% to 11.2%. However, the increase pales in comparison to changes in other provinces with Francophone populations, such as Manitoba (50.1% in 2001 and 55.5% in 2006) and Ontario (36.9% in 2001 and 41.8% in 2006).[31]

As a result of a recent Supreme Court decision (*Société des Acadiens et Acadiennes du Nouveau-Brunswick Inc. v. Canada* [2008]), the province's language rights appear to be far more encompassing than those provided by the federal Official Languages Act, given that services "must be made available in both English and French everywhere in the province regardless of the number of people who speak either language in a particular area. Services in both languages, moreover, must be of equal quality.[32] From this perspective, the federal Official Languages Act could be seen as the lowest common denominator that each province could improve upon in order to ensure the protection of their respective linguistic minorities. Nevertheless, and contrary to what has been the case in Quebec, it is important to note that while language rights are legally entrenched, this does not guarantee that they have been applied in reality. In New Brunswick, the francophone community is in many ways still disenfranchised and must persist in demanding that provincial authorities fully recognize their rights. Once again, the "push and pull" dynamic is at play and has led to a power imbalance between the francophone and anglophone communities.[33] The "pull" of English as a language of social mobility has meant that francophones in the province have a great difficulty in asserting themselves. This is evidence of the deleterious consequences of a language policy that advocates equal protection under the law.

Nunavut

Since its creation in 1999, the government of Nunavut has applied the Official Languages Act Revised Statutes of the North-West Territories 1988, which was amended in 1990 in order to provide official status to six indigenous languages (Cree, Slavey, Dogrib, Gwich'in, Chipweyan, and Inuktitut). This amendment was adopted in an attempt to counteract the decline of these regional languages and it has had a positive impact, contributing to a linguistic renaissance in Nunavut over the last two decades. In June 2007, two bills were presented in the Legislative Assembly that sought to provide equal legal status to English, French, and two Inuit languages (Inuktitut and Inuinaqtun).

Bill 6, adopted in June 2008 by the Nunavut Assembly and confirmed by the federal government on 11 June 2009, constitutes the new Official Languages Act and recognizes the equal status of French, English, and the Inuit languages in courts, the Legislative Assembly, and public services. The enshrinement of Bill 6 marks the first time that a language other than English and French has been given official status in Canada. This is landmark event for Canada's First Nations.

The primary objective of the Inuit Language Protection Act (Bill 7) is to protect, promote, and sustain the use of the Inuit language by affirming that it is an essential component of Inuit culture and history.[34] Bill 7, adopted by the Nunavut Assembly in September 2008, protects the use of the Inuit language as a language of instruction from kindergarten to the third grade, provides for the creation of an organization designed to "expand the knowledge and expertise available with respect to the Inuit Language, and to consider and make decisions about Inuit Language use, development and standardization under this Act,"[35] to protect the use of the Inuit language in the public sector and at the municipal level, and to ensure the right of instruction in the Inuit language is protected at all levels.[36]

Twenty years after the adoption of the Official Languages Act Revised Statutes of the North-West Territories, Nunavut is facing a similar situation to the one that francophone Québécois faced forty years ago.[37] The 2010 Nunavut Language Summit adopted the slogan "Our language brings us together" and, in doing so, provided evidence of a national group asserting its identity by rallying around the protection and promotion of a minority language. The Summit noted a significant decline in the use of the Inuit language: "In the 2006 census only 64% of Inuit in Nunavut reported speaking Inuktitut at home. This reflects a 10% decline from the 1996 census which found 76% spoke it at home."[38] The "pull" of the English language constitutes the greatest challenge to the survival of this community's linguistic identity.[39] I will argue in chapter 5 that the new constitutional dynamic in Canada and a changing global context provides the First Nations with greater opportunities to advance their claims and to force majority groups, in both Canada and Quebec, to exhibit greater sensitivity to precarious conditions for the persistence of indigenous cultures and languages.

Catalonia

In post-Franco Spain, it has been possible for national groups to regain the right to use their own languages. Benefiting from a national policy that recognized historic nations, the Catalan have adopted a series of important structural measures. The success of the Catalan people has in large part been due to the fact that they have been able to ensure their recognition as a historical nationality with nominal status as an autonomous region, and due to their particularly strong economy, which has been able to penetrate international markets. By following these two paths (economic and identitary), the Catalan people have been able to revitalize their language and to assert their role in this policy realm.

The new Constitution of 1978 enshrined Castilian as the state's official language, whereas all other principal spoken languages where given official status within their respective autonomous communities.

This created a problem in Catalonia, given that the region's citizens were under no obligation to learn Catalan; thus, it was difficult to impose the latter as the region's common public language. It was only in 1983 that Catalan was recognized as an official language. This recognition engendered greater cohesion within Catalonia's political and civil society institutions and, concomitantly, made Catalan the language of common citizenship and social inclusion. Moreover, Catalan is the pillar upon which Catalonia's specific citizenship regime is founded (see chapter 3).

The expansion of the European Union has also contributed to the consolidation of Catalan, given that a multitude of minority languages have a presence in supranational institutions. In other words, the new Spain – that is to say, a state undergoing a process of federalization – and the European Union – a hybrid federal/confederal arrangement – have both contributed to making Catalan a language that is both attractive and useful. Catalan is the eighth most spoken language in the European Union.[40]

In their attempts to promote linguistic diversity in Spain, the Catalan people have adopted several components of Quebec's language policy. The collaborative ties between the government of Quebec and Catalonia's Generalitat are particularly strong and are evidenced, in part, by the signing in 1996 of l'Entente de coopération en matière linguistique entre le gouvernement du Québec et le gouvernement autonome de la Catalogne.[41] This agreement is centred on the exchange of information over the measures adopted ·in Quebec and Catalonia to protect each state/region's respective language and evaluations of these measures.

In 1983, Catalonia's Generalitat promulgated its own Linguistic Normalization Law, which established that Catalan was the *lengua propria de Catalunya* (the language specific to Catalonia), and in 1998 the Law on Language Policy: both of these laws were modelled after Quebec's language policy. The government of Quebec has also, in its desire to promote the cause of minority languages on the global scale, exchanged information with Catalan authorities on how to collect and manage data.

More recently, the Catalan government had made an important advance in language policy by making "Catalan the primary language employed by the public administration and media" operating within the borders of the autonomous region. However, this new legislation was declared unconstitutional by the Constitutional Court of Spain on 28 June 2010. This new approach to language policy would have been beneficial for the future of Catalonia even more so given that the future of the Catalan language is uncertain. By all appearances, Catalan is at a greater risk of disappearing than is French in Canada.

~ೞ~⁔

In Canada, francophones and the First Nations have benefited from the popularity of claims based on the discourse of individual and collective rights and have been able to assert, little by little, their presence within a multinational state (that, ironically, is reticent to recognize this fact). Both cases demonstrate the inextricable link between national identity and political legitimacy that is central to the existence and survival of multinational states.

The presence of a federal society has helped to provide legitimacy to minority nations who, in return, have sought to provide members of their respective societies with a "context of choice"[42] in order to ensure both their full actualization and the deepening of democratic practices. This does not signify, by any means, that the survival of these nations is guaranteed: the overwhelming size of the anglophone population in the Northern Hemisphere and the "pull" of the English language are daunting forces. As we are reminded by Kenneth McRoberts: "So, Canada [is] more than ever a multi-national state in terms of its underlying social and cultural reality. Yet, it's also more than ever a nation-state in its dominant discourse and political institutions."[43] For Canada to be truly multinational, the Canadian federal system would have to cater to the needs of minority nations and the national government would have to stop viewing federalism "as a mean by which a single national community can divide and diffuse power."[44]

In light of the preceding reflections, we must ask ourselves a few important questions. Is the central government truly capable of upholding and defending the fundamental principles of federalism? In what way are federal entities capable of providing their citizens with a context of choice that allows them to develop an authentic dialogue between their territorial identity and the values that cut across the polity? How can the founding nations of a federation emancipate themselves politically, culturally, socially, and economically? These questions must be addressed and answered through the development of governmental policies that respond to the needs of minority nations.

Federalism may offer the means to promote minority languages and to ensure their long-term survival. It is a necessary but insufficient condition for the effective and just management of diversity. First, despite having the tools at their disposal to preserve their language, minority nations will always find themselves in a context where they are surrounded by a majority language: English in Nunavut and Quebec, and Spanish in Catalonia. Second, English is the global lingua franca and exercises a strong "pull" at the international level.

I conclude this chapter by noting the unfortunate irony that in attempting to preserve their respective languages, minority nations must invariably make their case in English if they hope to advance their claims on the international scene.

2 New Challenges for Multinational States: Globalization and Competing Citizenship Regimes[1]

It is by adopting values, prioritizing them and specifying their outcomes that human beings structure their existence, exercise their judgment and guide their conduct.

Gérard Bouchard and Charles Taylor[2]

In and of itself, one phenomenon – globalization – has markedly contributed to the uncertain future of minority nations. Indeed, globalization is one of the foremost threats to the continued existence and growth of minority nations. In 2014, this threat is more important than ever as the economic benefits of globalization are almost uncontested, while the negative cultural impacts of this phenomenon are all but ignored.

One of the deleterious effects of globalization comes in the form of how the concept has been appropriated by officials in the governments of multination states. Political elites who work at the heart of the central governments have used the phenomenon of ·"globalization" as a pretext to alter the balance of power between the latter and the constitutive entities of multinational federations. These elites argue that globalization requires the centralization of power in order to ensure efficient decision-making. In turn, "efficiency" has become synonymous with the continued disenfranchisement of minority nations in the multinational state. Within this context, it behoves us to assess the impact of these challenges and to find innovative ways to redeploy democratic institutions in order to respond to them in a legitimate manner. Failing to do so, we run the risk of witnessing the erosion of democracy and differentiated citizenship regimes in countries that are marked by deep communal diversity.[3]

So this chapter has two purposes. The first is to show to what extent globalization has deleterious consequences with regard to the democratic treatment of minority nations, but also to shed some positive light on how globalization has opened up new avenues for "nations without states" to advance their political claims. The second purpose of this chapter is to argue that states need to respond to threats, like that of globalization, with an openness to experiment with plurinational models of governance that can establish citizenship regimes capable of accommodating deep diversity. To be sure, some may retort that such an approach could breed instability. I respond, however, that questions of political stability should cede the way to issues of transparency as it relates to decision-making and the quest for recognition and justice within and among a federation's constitutive units.[4] I will argue that political stability is, in fact, the natural by-product of an equitable and just society where diversity is affirmed and recognized. Thus, under the auspices of globalization, politics should lead to the deepening of liberal democratic values and not to interventionism with the goal of simply sustaining dominant socio-political institutions.[5] In other words, our approach to governance and citizenship must evolve in order for minority nations to be able to thrive in a world of globalization.

Globalization

Globalization is not a recent development; rather it is a political phenomenon that has been on an upward trend over the past several centuries. It has manifested itself in different ways, including economic imperialism, the transnational adoption and implementation of capitalism, the dissemination of knowledge through patents and blueprints, the process of acculturation, and, more specific to the context at hand, the erosion of linguistic diversity and the concomitant enshrinement of a global lingua franca. The works of linguist Claude Hagège confirm this deleterious impact of globalization. "Akin to civilizations, languages are also mortal and the abyss of history is deep enough to digest both. However, dead languages have unusual properties ... They can be resurrected! Nonetheless, we must be vigilant. The survival of many languages, including French, is threatened."[6]

Contemporary globalization has brought into question the importance of the state and has levelled the playing field between the state and other actors, including corporations and social movements. This new tendency suggests that the state no longer has a responsibility to intervene in the market to ensure its domestication or to assume the mantle of leadership over the redistribution of collective goods, nor does it have a duty to maintain the necessary conditions for the enrichment of the diverse communities sharing national and supranational spaces. Political and economic actors, for whom the persistence of market efficiency trumps all other socio-political concerns, often dismiss the aforementioned consequences of globalization.[7] For some corporate actors it is of the utmost importance to ensure that social progress does not offset economic gains. In sum, economic, cultural, and technological transnational phenomena have further eroded state sovereignty. The increased importance of economic actors within socio-political spaces – which are continually in the process of being reconfigured – has come with a decline in the ability of nation states to exercise what was once an exclusive jurisdictional control over her territories.[8]

An Example of the Globalization's Impact: The Cotonou Agreement

The Cotonou Agreement, signed by the member states of the European Union and the African, Caribbean, and Pacific Group of States (ACP) on 23 June 2000, evidences both a new globalist and neoliberal approach despite the fact that the language of the agreement evokes the principles of solidarity and openness to others.

According to Raoul Marc Jennar, political scientist and member of Unité de Recherche, de Formation et d'Information sur la Globalization, "the European Union has decided to impose the rules of the World Trade Organization (WTO) on the counties of the ACP in lieu of opting for a closer and more equitable relationship. In turn, it has decided that the least developed countries (LDCs) of the ACP (40 out of 77) will lose special dispensations provided to them by the WTO if they opt not to sign free-trade agreements."[9] In an attempt to quell potential opposition to the agreement, the EU opted to negotiate individual agreements with countries on a territorial basis. These agreements, known as Economic Partnership Agreements (EPA) and compatible with the rules of the World Trade Organization, evidence the adoption of a divide-and-conquer strategy. Negotiations for the EPAs began in 2003 and, according to Jennar, are particularly troubling for the survival of the African Francophonie:

> The Commission, the negotiator for the European Union's member states, has imposed the language, content and rhythm of negotiations in spite of

protests from governments of the ACP countries. Furthermore, English is the language of discussion and documents are also written in English. Paradoxically, French is the dominant language for 94% of the total combined population of ACP countries. However, the Union has opted to focus on the fact that only 20 of 48 African countries have French as an official language.[10]

Organizations such as Third World Network Africa have denounced these practices by describing "EPAs ... as tools of European domination over developing markets."[11] These practices are both scandalous and troubling in relation to the persistence of French in European and international organizations. The impact of these types of practices is not limited to French-speaking countries; they have also had a deleterious effect on countries with deep linguistic cleavages (such as Spain).

Constructing Europe

In the context of the construction of Europe, we must ask ourselves whether the installation and development of a supranational government threatens the sovereignty of its member states and, by extension, the 77 countries of the ACP. The construction of Europe entailed four outcomes: (1) the commodification of markets with little respect for less developed nations; (2) the centralization of power in Brussels and Strasbourg; (3) the cross-polity imposition of "neutral" legal norms; (4) the ascension of English as the uncontested language of prestige and the concomitant retreat of national languages from international and supranational organizations. In this new context, once dominant languages are at risk of losing their international dimension; the decreased use of French during economic and social summits and during international sporting events, such as the Olympics, is but one example of this phenomenon.

Economic globalization has also led to the development of disturbing practices within both the European Union and its member states. For example, decision-makers have opted to reduce the level of social services offered to Europeans, so we are told, in order to increase interstate competitiveness by opening up the market to more than a handful of states.[12] This is how it goes; new public policies more attuned to corporate growth than they are with the need to enshrine solidarity and to attenuate the side-effects of cutthroat competition, as well as to entrench a just citizenship regime.[13]

In brief, proponents of neoliberalism see international competition as an objective in of itself; for an investor, choosing one language over another is an economic calculation tied to the profit margin and the choice is often made without considering its potentially destructive impact on the social fabric of a polity. Furthermore, this school of thought often sees language as a "cost" rather than as a "benefit." This was the case in Canada, where manufacturers opposed the printing of labels in two languages by invoking its costliness. What, then, if language is an integral part of a rich culture and not simply an economic asset? What if language policy provides a means to redress social inequality across large economic entities? Québécois have attempted to provide answers to these questions over the last half-century,[14] all the while developing a rich literature on participatory citizenship.

As we have seen, it is all too often the case that the modern state is too focused on increasing its margins of profit and on opening up new economic markets. In order to do so, the state and industry have opted to cut social programs for employees. This decision has, in turn, led to the deterioration of work conditions. In brief, we see here the adherence to the golden rule of economic productivity, while the social outcomes of this of this focus on profits are overlooked.

Given this tunnel vision, the state has sought to eliminate burdens on new investors and to reduce tax rates for big and small businesses. Having done so, the state has witnessed the decline of its capacity to intervene, extract, and redistribute with legitimate authority. Paradoxically, while the state's redistributive role is eroding, the number of impediments to adopting beneficial social and economic projects is increasing exponentially. In this world of "every man for himself," we must emphasize the need for national groups to form a united front in response to economic determinism and its impact on culture and politics.[15]

Competing Citizenship Regimes

Modern states are often called upon to intervene in the deployment of citizenship regimes. Within this context, the pillars of "inclusion" and "exclusion" have become the barometers by which one can assess public policies adopted in response to globalization.[16] Unfortunately, problems of "exclusion" are being poorly addressed. In fact, political actors are prone to invoke globalization as a reason for the state's retreat from processes of social equalization.

In the works of Jane Jenson and Susan Phillips,[17] the "citizenship regime" is an important concept that helps to distinguish between national communities within multinational states. This concept transcends categories of "gender," "territory," and "class," all the while incorporating them into an encompassing explanatory framework. According to Jenson, the citizenship regime is a by-product of political struggle and

> is taken to denote the institutional arrangements, rules and understandings that guide and shape concurrent policy decisions and expenditures of the state, problem definitions by states and citizens, and claims-making by citizens. As such, a citizenship regime encodes within it a paradigmatic representation of multidimensional political identities, of the "national" as well as the "model citizen," of the "second-class citizen," and of the non-citizen. It also encodes representations of the proper and legitimate social relations among and within these categories, as well as the borders between "public" and "private."[18]

Being a multinational state,[19] Canada is a particularly interesting case in the context of the current discussion because it contains two citizenship regimes that recognize civic, communal, political, and social rights for each citizen within distinct political spaces. Within this context, Canada's two distinct host societies have adopted different models of social integration, cultural identification, and political representation: multiculturalism and interculturalism.[20] Despite their differences, these two citizenship regimes constitute spaces of liberty where democracy serves as an effective arbiter of individual rights. Quebec's citizenship regime – as well as those of Catalonia, Scotland, and Wallonia[21] – can offer useful insight for other minority nations in negotiating their relationship with majority nations and for nation states interacting with supranational organizations.

Recognizing and Revealing Political Communities

The concept of the citizenship regime brings to light three dimensions of the process of identity building: the exercise of rights, belonging, and access to institutions.[22] These elements are essential for the representation of the political subject. However, they have little to say about the recognition of societal diversity – from which the polis derives its legitimacy – by political actors.[23]

The recognition of minority communities at the regional and state level is too often seen as the outcome of a quest for privilege and the fulfilment of national self-interest. It is within this context that demands made by both federalist and autonomist factions in Quebec from the 1960s onwards have most of the time been deemed baseless or illegitimate. The federal government's refusal to recognize national diversity has, in turn, undermined its capacity to legitimately represent the ensemble of national communities living within its territory.[24]

For the last forty years, political parties and civil society in Quebec have been involved in a political project to deepen democracy that is without parallel in the Western world. This project has entailed the establishment of the Bélanger-Campeau Commission on the future of Quebec in 1990, the articulation of the sovereignty issue on electoral platforms, and the provincial government's decision to hold referenda (in May 1980 and October 1995) on Quebec's future within or outside of the Canadian federation. In fact, it is thanks to the 1995 referendum that political forces in Quebec were able to highlight the province's citizenship regime, to rally people under its banner, to show how it is morally defensible, and to demonstrate its potential as the lynchpin for the creation of a new state and its acceptance in the brotherhood of nation states.

By examining the political behaviour of Québécois, of whom 94 per cent had turned out to vote in the referendum, field research conducted in 1995–6 brought to light the fundamental features of the societal project promulgated by the Quebec government. Data demonstrated that support for sovereignty was largely based on the institutionalization of a politics of pluralism, the promotion of economic solidarity, and the actualization of a socially progressive agenda.[25]

The impetus for the referendum was the result of the coalescence of several factors: (1) an unwillingness on the part of Canadian's constitutional partners to recognize Quebec as a nation in its own right; (2) a central government that was increasingly inclined to trample on areas of provincial jurisdiction by invoking the need for it to respond to the deleterious consequences of globalization; (3) opposition to the Québécois vision of federalism based on the use of French as a common public language and the respect of national difference.

Since Quebec's second referendum, the federal government has yet to recognize the province's distinct political project. To be clear, in 2006 the federal government opted to recognize Quebec as a nation within a unified Canada. However, this has had little if any real-world impact.[26]

For the moment, political factions at the federal and provincial levels are more interested in the day-to-day management of their respective polity than they are in re-examining the division of powers and jurisdictional authority and in implementing a true federal culture within the country.[27]

Instead of attempting to imagine new ways for national communities to live together, federal political actors act as if the "Quebec question" has already been answered. Ironically, surveys conducted by the federal government confirm that 40 per cent of Quebec voters support the sovereignty option and that a noticeable portion of this support comes from the province's ethno-cultural communities.[28]

The federal government's decision to exclude the premier of Quebec from the Summit of the Americas in 2000, despite the fact that the Summit was held in the province, is another indication of the former's reticence to acknowledge the latter. The exclusion was all the more troubling given that Quebec was the only region/state (among and within the thirty-four states represented at the Summit) where francophones are the majority people.

We must bring into question the practices by which national governments exclude national minorities from decision-making and deliberative processes. This exclusion constitutes a refusal to acknowledge difference and, in turn, opens the door for protest and resistance from within minority nations and contributes to a shift away from the politics of conciliation and towards the politics of secession.[29] It also leads to the impoverishment of diversity and makes it impossible to conceptualize deep difference within a multinational context.

Developed liberal democracies must be open to new ideas and must be willing to experiment with plurinational models of governance. Whether these models are plurinational or consociational in nature, what is most important is that states be imaginative and open to the legitimate demands of national minorities and, in doing so, show that they are fulfilling the promise of democracy.[30] The idea is not necessarily to fundamentally reshape national minorities and the overarching units that they belong to. It is instead to provide a context that allows for the development of their societal projects and that reinforces their desire to deepen democracy. In the absence of such a context, the whole world is at risk, threatened by the imposition of uniform social and economic practices, by the homogenization of cultures and traditions, and by the decline of politics.

Towards a Social State

Citizenship regimes are rooted in different statist traditions. Naturally, the state is not a panacea for all societal problems, nor is the market economy, which is incapable of offering equitable solutions across the board. Nonetheless, in a world marked by economic competition, it is important to endow the state with sufficient power that it may direct market outputs towards the enrichment of society. The state must also continue its important role in the institutionalization of national diversity in accordance with the criteria of recognition, empowerment, and the quest for justice. We shall return to these ideas in the following chapter.

Today, the fabric of liberal democratic societies is threatened by new forms of social exclusion and political alienation[31] and by a state that is at the service of the economic imperatives of globalization and that has, in turn, too often abandoned its commitment to the protection of social rights.

It is in response to this troubling new international context that I argue that it is essential to re-conceptualize the state and to develop new citizenship regimes that are sensitive to the needs of national minorities demanding recognition. David Cameron and Janice Stein's idea of the *social investment state* – which should replace the neoliberal state – is a step in the right direction.[32] We must ask ourselves whether states have erred in embracing a transnational economy and whether we must take steps to respond to the challenges that continue to erode the legitimacy of political regimes and that impede progress towards social justice. Ideally:

> Cities that work – where pollution is low, crime is not a threat to safety, where neighbourhoods thrive, where communities cohere, where schools teach – make good economic sense ... The case for including the socially excluded is more than economic ... In a Social Investment State, policy is justified in social as well as economic terms and leaders seek to balance needs. Some of the resources generated by the expanding economy would be dedicated to support those unable to participate directly in its functioning.[33]

Debates on questions of identity, especially in situations of deep diversity, must therefore address the issue of enshrining differentiated citizenship that accounts both for long-standing national minorities and new waves of immigration. As we will see in the following chapter, this will require both the expansion and deepening of democratic practices and the entrenchment of active citizenship.

~~~

While this chapter has been critical with regard to the effects of globalization on minority nations, it is also forward looking, and optimistic about solutions that can be implemented to ensure that the future of these nations need not be uncertain. I have argued that the benefits of globalization and economic integration have been exaggerated without addressing their destructive impact on our social fabric. Now, more than ever, nation states have a vested interest in responding to globalization with a revival of the principles of federalism in order to achieve greater social justice and social cohesion.

Nation states rooted in the monist tradition find themselves in an increasingly untenable situation. The homogenizing logic that once facilitated the foundation of nation states and the spread of the Westphalian model has grown counter-productive over time: it now leads to an erosion of national diversity and to the impoverishment of democratic practices and institutions. The impact on national languages may be even more devastating,[34] and it is not hard to envision a world wherein linguistic diversity becomes the stuff of legend.[35] To be clear, the threat to national languages is not limited to minority languages. The consolidation of supranational institutions also threatens the languages of nation states that belong to such institutions. Leaders of nation states therefore have a vested interest in ensuring the survival of their respective languages and, by extension, their cultures, institutions, and identities. However, as argued in this chapter, these leaders must also be open to the implementation of a new citizenship regime that is based on plurinationality and that recognizes and celebrates deep difference. Nation states can yet become the flag-bearers of national, linguistic, and cultural diversity.

3 The Pillars of Quebec's New Citizenship Regime: The Informal Constitution and Interculturalism[1]

Any movement toward partnership [in Canada] must take into account the following facts. Two distinct societies are housed within a single country, and each has its own citizenship regime.

Jane Jenson[2]

With the release of the Parekh report in Britain[3] and the Bouchard-Taylor report in Quebec,[4] it behoves us to imagine new ways of living together in multinational states such as Canada, Spain, and the United Kingdom. Intercultural dialogue became a rallying cry in Europe with the publication of the *White Paper on Intercultural Dialogue: Living Together as Equals in Dignity*,[5] so much so that Europe even chose to name 2008 the year of intercultural dialogue. The intercultural project has also made an appearance in Japan, where scholars and public intellectuals have begun to explore the links between globalization and conviviality; the works of Miyoko Tsujimura are at the forefront of this new movement.[6]

These developments signal that we must incorporate a new dimension in addressing the plight of minority nations. Though we must not lose sight of the importance of institutional arrangements that affirm communal and individual rights, today we must focus on the nature of inter-communal relationships within the plurinational context. We must explore and address the tensions between national communities as well as the dynamics of *intra*-national communitarian tensions. Only in so doing can we enshrine the new form of citizenship regime outlined in chapter 2. However, we must not lose sight of the past and the importance of history when designing a model meant to persist over time nor should we imagine unrealistic or unattainable solutions, lest the drive for accommodation and reconciliation in modern democracies lose what little steam it has gained in recent years.

By now, the reader will have noticed that the unrealized identitary issues in Quebec, Catalonia, and Scotland are inextricably linked to each polity's association with a larger socio-political entity: Quebec with the Canadian federation, Catalonia with Spain, and Scotland with the United Kingdom. The realization of the institutional projects of each of these minority nations requires that they must, to borrow Joseph Yvon Thériault's expression, "make society."[7] In each case, the unfettering of popular sovereignty is a necessary condition for "making society" and, concomitantly, for the enshrinement of a new citizenship regime.

In this chapter, I will focus primarily on Quebec's evolutionary path within the Canadian federation. Here, I invoke the idea of the "informal constitution" as a tool of political empowerment and reflect on the best way of promoting active citizenship among and within the constitutive nations of the Canadian multinational state. To be clear, Quebec has yet to provide its consent to the constitutional reform of 1982. This decision has proved to be a significant impediment to full and equitable collaboration between Quebec and the federal government, and it has contributed to the lack of confidence and reciprocity between political institutions in Quebec and Canada as a whole. Nonetheless, this has not and should not prevent Quebec from establishing new institutions and from asserting its identity within the Canadian federation. We have seen the concomitant processes of institutional and identity building play out through a series of public inquiries, such as the Commission Proulx's investigation on the place of religion in public schools (1999), the Commission Larose's examination of the future of the French language in Quebec (2001), the États généraux sur la réforme des institutions démocratiques (the Estates General on the Reform of the Democratic Institutions, 2002–3), and the Commission Bouchard-Taylor on the practice of reasonable cultural and religious accommodation (2007).

These investigations have also revealed that Quebec must continue to renew, deepen, and consolidate bonds of trust among the province's diverse communities. However, this can only be accomplished under the province's informal constitution and despite the federal government's consistent overreaching into areas of provincial authority.[8] One the major challenges to the actualization of this project is the fact that, while the Canadian constitution recognizes multiculturalism, the inherent rights of First Nations, the rights of francophones outside of

Quebec, and the rights of Quebec's anglophone minority, the province's intercultural model has yet to be constitutionally enshrined. The current state of affairs undermines the facticity of French in Quebec as an identity, as a focal point for cross-cultural dialogue, and feeds the discussion and contestation in economic, political, and social arenas.

The only way to remedy the current state of affairs is through the institutionalization of true multinational federalism. This would provide Canada's two major national communities with the opportunity to implement their own national models within their respective territories. As argued in chapter 2, these models would have to respect and enshrine deep diversity, advance the cause of indigenous rights, embrace a redistributive ethic, and develop viable and self-managing host societies. In the pages that follow, I outline the major tenets of the Québécois model – interculturalism – and examine the impediments to its actualization.

Deepening and Expanding the "Informal Constitution"

Although Quebec does not have its own formal constitution, as argued elsewhere by Raffaele Iacovino and Michel Seymour,[9] it has nonetheless succeeded at adopting organic laws that, despite being incomplete, provide significant structure to guarantee its political future.[10] These laws – such as the Charte de la langue française, Charte des droits et libertés de la personne, Loi sur la consultation populaire, Loi sur le financement des partis politiques, and the Loi sur l'exercice des droits fondamentaux et des prérogatives du peuple québécois et de l'État du Québec – have given Quebec a political status that is unequalled by any other federal sub-unit in any other federal polity. This status has been reinforced by the federal government's symbolic recognition of the Québécois nation during the thirty-ninth legislature, which has opened the door for Quebec to assert its presence on the international scene and, in doing so, act in a manner consistent with the perception that the province is indeed a "state."[11]

Steps must be taken to recognize, expand, and deepen the province's informal constitution so that its constitutive components derive cross-cultural support[12] and that it all provides the overarching framework that governs governmental–societal relations. The legitimization of the informal constitution can also help to reify the province's intercultural model for managing diversity. According to the

Bouchard-Taylor commission, the intercultural model comprises five interrelated components:

> To summarize, let us say that Québec interculturalism a) institutes French as the common language of intercultural relations; b) cultivates a pluralistic orientation that is concerned with the protection of rights; c) preserves the necessary creative tension between diversity, on the one hand, and the continuity of the French-speaking core and the social link, on the other hand; d) places special emphasis on integration and participation; and e) advocates interaction.[13]

According to jurist Stephen Tierney, creating and legitimizing an informal constitution requires adopting a multilevel strategy. First, according Tierney, within a multinational federal context, federal subunits must continue to assert devolved powers and, at every opportunity, question and contest the national and international intrusion into their jurisdictional arenas. This dual approach creates space for the entrenchment of the informal constitutional framework.

Second, as James Tully contends, it is essential that a multinational state recognize the right of self-determination for all of its constitutive nations without, however, authorizing these nations to initiate the process of self-determination. This fundamental commitment is necessary given that the environment that a polity's judicial branch must address and respond to changes in reaction to political crises, international conflicts, behind-the-scenes machinations, and political realignment.[14]

Drawing inspiration from ancient constitutionalism, Tully highlights several reasons that allow him to confirm that Quebec was not (at the moment of writing in 1998) living in a free and democratic federation. This argument is incontestable:

> The other members of the federation can impose constitutional amendments without its [Quebec's] consent. They can also arbitrarily block any negotiation aiming at the constitutional recognition of Quebec as a nation. In 1982, a constitutional amendment, the Constitution Act 1982, was introduced and imposed on Quebec without its consent and despite its clearly articulated opposition to the amendment. This manoeuvre not only violated a constitutional convention (*Quod omnes tangit*) ... it also violated the new amending formula that had been institutionalized by the Constitution Act of 1982. Later on, Quebec had exercised its right to initiate

constitutional change by attempting to enshrine its identification as a "distinct society." The proposed amendment was blocked by one dissenting province and on the sole basis that the amending formula adopted in 1982 required the consent of all provinces. These two events demonstrate beyond a doubt that arbitrary limits are imposed on Quebec's right to negotiate the rules of its own recognition.[15]

Tully's assertion suggests that Quebec was in fact more free within the Canadian federation in the pre-1982 period, a period when political decisions were framed under the ambit of convention rather than a constitution.[16] Stephen Tierney supports this point of view when he argues: "It is of course widely argued that in Canada until 1982 a 'conventional', 'informal' or 'procedural' constitutional model prevailed wherein Quebec's status was not fully articulated in the text of the constitution. This allowed Quebec the opportunity to seek constitutional accommodation within a more loosely constituted federation by means of the unwritten conventions and practices which under-pinned it."[17] Tierney's words lead us to rethink the current state of affairs and to imagine that the entrenchment of an informal constitution would provide Quebec with greater freedom in policymaking than the formal constitution has thus far.

Third, Quebec must also play an active role in constitutional negotiations; they can legitimize a political process by bringing to light the demands and expectations of a variety of actors. This is what occurred in Quebec during the negotiations surrounding the Meech Lake Accord (1987–90), and this is also what happened in Catalonia during the process of public consultation in June 2006 leading up to the reformed version of the community's Statute of Autonomy.[18] These two processes contributed to the articulation of a common public identity in their respective nations that are, in turn, avenues for the deepening of social cohesion.

Fourth, political leaders must not hesitate to seek out and promote constitutional innovations that may not necessarily be de jure at the outset. For example, in Quebec, the modification of practices has sometimes been translated into de jure changes;[19] nowhere is this transformation more evident than in the realm of immigration policy.[20] Here, the British concept of finding and employing "abeyances" that underlie the constitution[21] as a means to revitalize conventional constitutionalism is particularly important for minority nations. Challenging constitutional norms through abeyances may be even more fruitful than seeking to create a common public culture,[22] given that, in the case of an abeyance, norms are contested and actualized without recourse to formal constitutionalism. The concept of abeyances fits well within Quebec's model of interculturalism, as will be shown later, since the latter denies the existence of a homogeneous or "common" society and, instead, brings cultural difference to the fore and highlights the tensions that underlie a political project that must continually attempt to "make society." Moreover, an intercultural approach assumes that collective action is the norm, something that cannot be said about the common public culture approach. Finally, interculturalism recognizes the importance and tolerates the existence of dissenting voices in order to prevent the complete erosion of a basic shared identity.

We can see, then, that Quebec's approach to the recognition and protection of identity has differed significantly from Canadian multiculturalism. The drive for the enshrinement of interculturalism is a legitimate right of Quebec by virtue of the fact that it is a liberal society and also a foundational pillar of Canada's multinational federation. Nevertheless, the federal government has attempted to reframe and restrain this initiative and, concomitantly, impose its norms on Québécois. This has meant the promulgation, by national political institutions and agencies, of a monist model of governance in spite of and in opposition to differentiated political bodies that are the legitimate products of a federal political system. Under these conditions, only one course of action can be advocated: abandon the monist conception of sovereignty and, as Geneviève Nootens argues, embrace the idea that a polity is constituted of a plurality of communities of belonging. The idea of the multinational state is the embodiment of this new framework.[23]

So long as we remain in a monist scenario, we will continue to witness the confrontation between two nation-building projects, each attempting to impose their own values at the expense of the other. Given that the different orders of government have different means at their disposal, it is easy to see that the national majority can, with greater facility, impose its will on Quebec as a national minority.[24] As Donald Forbes argues:

> Multiculturalism and separatism (or national unity) are often treated as if they were unrelated topics … But a glance at the origins of Canada's official multiculturalism suffices to show the artificiality of this scholarly separation between two closely related topics: official multiculturalism was obviously, at its inception, part of a national unity strategy, that is,

part of a plan to weaken and eventually to defeat the separatist movement in Quebec.[25]

While the federal government has provided tangible support to many of the country's cultural minorities, it has also attempted to corral all identitary issues under its sole jurisdiction and, in doing so, has been the lynchpin of opposition to Quebec's struggle for national affirmation. This approach is anathema to the concretization of a relationship of confidence between Quebec and the rest of Canada.

Interculturalism, Active Citizenship, and the New "Vivre-Ensemble"

The reasonable-accommodation debate and the release of the Bouchard-Taylor report (2008) have brought to light the need to revisit and, perhaps, re-conceptualize the Québécois idea of "vivre-ensemble." By doing so it reconnects with René Lévesque's take on this very issue at accommodating significant others: Traditionally, academics and politicians have focused on how the province's major communities (francophones, anglophones, First Nations) and, more recently, "allophones" negotiate their differences in order to cohabitate with one another.[26] However, the contentious debate over the limits of cultural accommodation for (primarily) Muslims and Orthodox Jews that spurred the creation of the Bouchard-Taylor commission suggests that we must now add an intra-community dimension to this discussion. Within this context there are three major steps that need to be taken in order to reconcile inter- and intra-community negotiations and to develop a new "vivre ensemble."

First, the examination of intra-community tensions must take into consideration the fact that diversity within Quebec has and, for the foreseeable future, will be framed within the context of federal–provincial (or centre–periphery) relations. It is essential to note that the Canadian constitution has enshrined multiculturalism and has failed to recognize the development of an "intercultural" model in Quebec. In effect, the constitutionalization of multiculturalism undermines the primary facets of Québécois identity with the intercultural model, notably: the facticity of French and the significant overlap between cultural, economic, political, and social concerns. The only way to reconcile the coexistence of these two distinct models is through the entrenchment of de jure multinational federalism. The advent of true multinational federalism would allow the country's two national communities to enshrine distinct models that, nonetheless, converge on a respect for deep diversity, the promulgation of indigenous rights, the protection of individual rights, and the redistribution of public goods.

Second, the development of multinational federalism requires that the monistic conceptualization of national sovereignty cede way, both at the federal and provincial levels, to the idea of enshrining plural communities of belonging. As long as monist conceptualizations of sovereignty persist, we will find ourselves in a situation where two parallel national projects compete with each other in an attempt to impose their respective core values on the province's constituency.

Third, and most important, the intercultural model must be developed with an eye to remedying some of the failures of Canadian multiculturalism. To be clear, many liberal democracies have developed models for dealing with diversity in response to claims for cultural and linguistic recognition and the sub-state affirmation of group identity. Most of these models have been proposed as means to redress socio-economic disparities between ethnic communities and national majorities and as mechanisms for restoring citizen confidence in political institutions. Examples of these models are the Spanish autonomous state system, the consociational arrangements of several small European states,[27] "territorial federalism" (e.g., the United States), binational or multinational federalism (e.g., Belgium), and the idiosyncratic Canadian model, which is a hybrid of territorial federalism and de facto multinationalism.[28] While these models have ensured some degree of national political stability, they have not stopped academics from challenging their validity and they have not prevented minority groups from adopting their own means of dealing with difference. In Canada, this has entailed the development of a critical discourse on multiculturalism and of a conceptual dichotomy between national multiculturalism and Québécois interculturalism.

Multiculturalism is typically presented, outside of Quebec, as the norm for dealing with diversity, and as the locus of Canada's evolving and mutable national identity. However, multiculturalism has come under increased scrutiny. A number of scholars have come to argue that multiculturalism is "ethnicizing" social relations; Daiva Stasiulis, Yasmeen Abu-Laban, and Vince Wilson[29] contend that multiculturalism encourages the juxtaposition of groups[30] and that it may even harm the integration of members of cultural communities into the Canadian family; and Charles Taylor has pointed out that multiculturalism is also part of a "passive" strategy for building Canadian citizenship. It is passive because multiculturalism has been reduced to the expression of a fact enshrined in the Canadian constitution instead of being the expression of specific practices resulting from the evolving interaction between groups and political communities.

In the wake of the Bouchard-Taylor commission, Canadian and Québécois academic and political discourses have turned their attention to the differences between multicultural and intercultural approaches. In contrast to what is suggested by the multicultural model in Québéc, interculturalism proposes the enshrinement of an ever-evolving form of active citizenship channelled through various institutions including government commissions, political parties, trade unions, and civic organizations. Interculturalism does not require members of cultural minorities to merge into a larger whole. Rather the model requires the public expression of differences and seeks to democratize decision-making by revealing majority or aggregate political preferences.

Quebec's interculturalism reveals a deep commitment to political transformation. It gives meaning to the public sphere as a space for major cultural, economic, political, and social negotiation and provides an opportunity for the creation of closer links between constituent preferences and the design and implementation of public policy. In doing so, interculturalism offers an alternative to accepting the imposed and (relatively) non-negotiable and immutable national institutional framework. Quebec's intercultural model also strikes a balance between the recognition of cultures living within the province's boundaries and Québécois nation building. In other words, interculturalism enshrines both social solidarity and openness to diversity.

Some may argue that interculturalism's insistence on continual public debate is indicative of low levels of inter-communal trust. However, inter-communal exchanges and the creative tensions that give rise to these exchanges can also be a means of revealing trust as more people become willing to take part in deliberations and to freely express their preferences in a public forum. These interactions create opportunities for cross-cultural dialogue that can potentially promote cross-community reconciliation and further the consolidation of social ties among diverse facets of the constituency. The establishment of a more concrete intercultural model both in Quebec and in other polities may also help to encourage the full participation of civil society actors and to avoid what Daniel Innerarity argues is the real impediment to the enshrinement of qualitative democracy: "Identity and Ideological confrontations do not necessarily pose a threat to democracy. The real threat is rather the lack of discussion, the pressure of unanimity, the imposition of political correctness, or the fact of building up the individual in a universal point of view that must be adopted by everyone."[31]

One avenue worth exploring would be the predominance of the Canadian Charter of Rights and Freedoms over the Quebec Charter of Human Rights and Freedoms. Were the lines of judicial authority be redrawn this would contribute to reinvigorate a federal ideal. However, as Charles Taylor suggests, relying solely on charters may lead to sacrifices at the political level. Guy Laforest summarizes this well when he says that "Taylor cautions those who swear by charters of rights and the safeguards they offer citizens. He reminds them that the vogue for charters can mean a withering away of political life, an estrangement of citizens from their public institutions in modern society."[32] In short, it is important to be mindful that charters, like all formal constitutions, do not represent a panacea because they can themselves contribute to the impoverishment of political life.

Another avenue could involve developing the idea of informal constitutionalism. This would allow for greater exploration of the federal principle of autonomy and non-subordination of powers.[33] Political actors in Canada continue to overlook this principle's potential for promoting more democratic and respectful forms of constitutionalism.

The Supreme Court of Canada also concluded, in the *Reference re the Secession of Quebec* (1998), that in Canada "[our] political and constitutional practice has adhered to an underlying principle of federalism, and has interpreted the written provisions of the Constitution in this light. For example, although the federal power of disallowance was included in the *Constitution Act, 1867*, the underlying principle of federalism triumphed early" (section 55).

Though it is debatable whether the Supreme Court's interpretation of the federal principle has been vigorously upheld through time, what matters most, in my opinion, is less the existence of the federal principle per se but its recognition. This principle provides a space whereby members of the Canadian federation can democratically assert themselves that should not be overlooked or underestimated – a space for them to advance claims and make communal demands.[34] This, in turn, establishes an informal constitution, as explored in the first part of this chapter, and thereby improves the relationship between the various national communities.

In summary, democracy must be founded on a trust that is conditional and reversible.[35] Such a condition makes it possible to think about a strong Quebec–Canada relationship that is open and frank. The health of democracy in Quebec and in Canada depends on their mutual commitment to such deliberation. In this sense, it has been shown that interculturalism is better suited than multiculturalism when it comes to noticing and addressing tensions between communities.

Fundamentally speaking, interculturalism provides a framework that allows citizens to actively engage in political life and participate in contemporary political institutions. The quality of the trust-based relationship depends primarily on the willingness of political and social actors to implement a vision of active citizenship rooted in an intercultural vision. Trust, in this sense, is therefore not given blindly or without conditions. On the contrary, it is consistently and openly tested and contested. To the extent that such a project can be realized and further strengthened, it will also become possible for political and social actors to promote and entrench the ideals discussed above.

4 From Containment to Empowerment: Moving towards Positive Autonomy[1]

Peoples never have more freedom than the degree to which their courage conquers fear.

Henri-Marie Beyle Stendhal (1783–1842)

In debates on decolonization, philosophers relied heavily on the works of Isaiah Berlin and, in particular, his distinction between negative and positive liberty. While this distinction yielded many debates among philosophers, comparativists largely overlooked these exchanges. In the pages that follow, I bring the concepts of negative and positive freedom into the discussion on minority nations and use it to shed new light on the realization of political autonomy in Canada, Spain, and multinational federations writ large.

For Berlin, negative liberty (i.e., freedom from) corresponds to the absence of constraints, interference, and domination, whereas positive liberty (i.e., freedom to) suggests an open-ended path for political action that can lay the groundwork for a politics of recognition and empowerment.

Over time, Berlin refined his notions of negative and positive freedom. He argued that negative freedom embodied a "possibility of action," whereas positive freedom entailed an "action in of itself."[2] He contended that "the essence of the notion of liberty, in both the 'positive' and the 'negative' senses, is the holding off of something or someone – of others who trespass on my field or assert their authority over me, or of obsessions, fears, neuroses, irrational forces – intruders and despots of one kind or another."

Although these forms of liberty are traditionally applied to the realm of individual rights, I contend that the conceptualization of positive liberty can also be applied to the rights of collectivities. Here, the collectivity corresponds to a people with an institutional identity and a national societal culture that provides a unique and distinct "context of choice."[3] If we accept this conceptual application, the best possible manifestation of positive freedom would entail the enshrinement of a right of external and internal self-determination for national groups.

At this juncture, it is important to invoke Philip Pettit's distinction between non-interference and liberty as a form of non-domination. This distinction will serve as a backdrop for the arguments made in this chapter.[4] In Pettit's words:

> It is possible to think of non-domination either as a goal that the state should promote or as a constraint that it should honour. In the first case, we think that the state should be designed so that expected non-domination among those who live under the system is at a maximum. In the second case, we think that it should be designed so that, whether or not expected non-domination is maximized, the system unambiguously testifies to the value of non-domination: this, through assuming the form required to promote expected non-domination in the ideally compliant world; this, in particular, through not involving the slightest taint of domination in the state's own constitutional arrangements.[5]

The manner in which Pettit goes about situating political relationships constitutes a significant advance. However, we must expand on his liberal republican perspective by focusing on the empowerment of national communities within multinational states. What is truly important is that nations be provided with the opportunity to be proactive in their quest for meaning.

Neither Berlin nor Pettit go so far as to conceptualize the empowering dimension of liberty: a form of liberty that allows political actors to engage in determining political action. Within this context, it is possible to contribute to the current debate on autonomy by exploring Canadian politics and, concomitantly, by dismissing the notion that the government of Quebec is not sufficiently proactive and that this is the result of dual fear of seeing its fate determined by the courts and/or of engendering animosity with Ottawa or other units of the federation (see chapter 3). My focus here is on the constraints that the government of Quebec imposes on itself voluntarily more so than on any real constraint imposed from without. In brief, the notion of *positive autonomy*, inspired by the works of Berlin and Pettit, asks us to rethink the contours of the autonomist project in order to enhance its emancipatory and empowering dimensions. It is useful to remind readers here of Charles Taylor's 1985 essay "What's Wrong with Negative Liberty," in which he explains that even defenders of negative liberty (in addition to positive libertarians of course) are forced to rely upon some basic degrees of understanding as to what activities and goals are significant to the self-realization of human beings. This enunciated particularly well the notion that is central to this chapter: the concept of empowerment.[6]

This chapter is divided into three sections. First, I focus on the challenges that Quebec is facing within the Canadian federation. Second, I examine the ways in which the government of Quebec has attempted to advance its claims in its struggle with the central government and, in some cases, other member states of the federation. Third, I identify new avenues for enhancing Quebec's freedom within the Canadian political space, all the while addressing Quebec's empowerment at the international level. This chapter provides useful lessons for other nations seeking recognition and empowerment and contributes to the current discussion on multination federalism and national diversity.[7]

The (Im)Balance of Power

Canada is conceptualized as a *negotiated country*[8] without the constraints present in other states where the rules of the game were imposed following a civil war (e.g., the United States), a conflict between armed forces (e.g., the Second World War), or in the wake of regime change (e.g., post-Franco Spain). Although one can argue that Canada is a negotiated country, political factions have been largely unresponsive to Quebec's autonomist claims since Confederation in 1867. Quebec's claims have only been the subject of any real discussion when they have impacted the functioning of the central state.

Andrée Lajoie reminds us that the central government possesses powers that allow it to shift the balance of power in its favour. Among these powers, *federal paramountcy* dictates that in a dispute over legal authority it is the central government that must prevail over the provincial jurisdiction.[9] Lajoie also points to the fact that *residual powers*, outlined in paragraph 29 of article 91 of the Constitution Act, are determined by the central government. In addition, the central government possesses certain pan-Canadian powers that give it the right to exercise its authority in extra-provincial domains (examples thereof include the central government's actions in relation to the public consumption of alcohol at the end of the nineteenth century and, more recently, in the realm of marine pollution).[10] Furthermore, the central government can also adopt special measures in response to political and economic crises or in response to insurrection or other forms of societal disturbances. The central government adopted several special measures over the course of the twentieth century.[11] According to François Chevrette and Herbert Marx, "Canada has been under some form emergency legislation for roughly 40% of the post–World War I era."[12] The central government has used other instruments to establish the rules of the game, including disallowance and reservation, declaratory power, the acquisition of public properties, and the federal spending power.[13]

Declaratory power allows the central government to expand its jurisdiction without the consent of the federation's member states in the name of acting on behalf of the well-being of the general population. This intrusive power was used 470 times, but has fallen into disuse since 1961. It was employed, inter alia, in the realms of interprovincial transportation, public transportation, the building of aqueducts, and creation of parks.[14] The declaratory power, in its design and application, is antithetic to the principle of federalism and to the division of powers between different orders of government.

The central government also acquired a vast array of public properties in the wake of the Second World War, when it was at its interventionist peak. The central government had full authority to intervene in this domain given its constitutionally enshrined rights over public property and because its capacity to intervene was enhanced by the weakened position of the country's member states in the three decades following the end of the war.[15] This right made the central government a key actor in urban and regional development and, in turn, antagonized the government of Quebec.

Among other areas, the central government opted to act outside of the constraints of the constitutional framework by frequently flexing its fiscal power. This non-constitutional power provides the central government with a high degree of manoeuvrability and has allowed it to impose conditions that member states must adhere to in order to have access to public funds. The central government has not hesitated to use this power to trample on the member states' authority in areas such as health policy, regional and municipal development, and education.[16]

All of these powers have contributed to centralizing power in Ottawa and to forcing member states to take a stand in an attempt to prevent a further decline of their autonomy. Paradoxically, while the Canadian federation is seen by many as one of the most decentralized polities in the world, we can nonetheless see that the balance of power favours the central government.

Containment and Contentment

In the wake of the second failed referendum in Quebec, a conference was held on the future of the Belgian and Canadian federations in December 1995, in Brussels. At this conference, Stéphane Dion articulated two strategies for ensuring the survival of federations. The first strategy entailed the containment, by a national majority, of the "divisive" elements in a union by promoting constituent identification with common goals and a shared identity. The second strategy required that the national majority respond favourably and naively to all demands advanced by sub-state rivals. This acquiescence or, in Dion's words, "politics of contentment," would satisfy unhappy elements in the polity and encourage a political culture where demands would be invariably met with concessions.[17]

This second strategy was presented as something to avoid, given that a politics of contentment would, according to Dion, never truly satisfy political factions whose primary goal was to exit the union. On the flip-side, this is how Dion, upon his entry in active politics, defined the defenders of a strategy of containment, or what is known as "Plan B":

> According to the tenets of containment, nationalists can not be contented: they need their own country. The more that you give them, the more they will demand, leading eventually to secession. Each new concession will allow them to mark off more of their territory, to define themselves as an increasingly exclusive "us," to further exclude the other group and to reject common institutions that are perceived as a threat to the nation and embodiments of a foreign entity.[18]

The central government's strategy of containment has been norm in Canada for the last forty years. It has been redeployed with greater emphasis in the wake of the 1980 and 1995 referenda. For example:

- The central government's repeated use of its spending power to impose Canadian norms and values on the member states;
- The imposition of a constitutional amending formula in 1982 that failed to recognize Quebec's historic veto right;[19]

- The adoption of a social union framework without Quebec's consent;[20]
- The adoption of a foreign policy that tramples on Quebec's jurisdiction;[21]
- The creation of a Canada-wide securities commission;[22]
- The use of public funds to advance Canadian unity and to promote the central government within Quebec's territory.[23]

Although containment has been the norm, there are a few notable exceptions to this pattern of action. During Lester B. Pearson's tenure as head of Liberal minority governments between 1963 and 1968, the central government was more conciliatory towards Quebec's demands and even endorsed the entrenchment of asymmetrical federalism.[24] In policy terms, this entailed the creation of the Quebec Pension Plan and the transfer of certain forms of taxation authority to Quebec.[25] A more recent example of this conciliatory approach occurred between 1984 and 1990 and included the Mulroney government's renewal of constitutional discussions in an attempt to reintegrate Quebec into the Canadian federation with *honour and enthusiasm*. The election of the Conservative party brought an end to a period of Liberal party dominance at the federal level (1963–84), a period that was interrupted in 1979 by Joe Clark's Conservative government and a concomitant responsiveness to provincial and regional claims making. During the Mulroney years, the government of Quebec was able to fully participate in the newly set up Sommet de la Francophonie.[26]

In recent years, the Harper Conservative government, in power since 2006, has promoted "open federalism."[27] This new form of federalism proposes to limit the central government's intrusion into provincial jurisdiction, to address the impact of the federal deficit on provincial autonomy, and to allow Quebec to play a more important role in the international arena, starting with providing it with a presence at UNESCO meetings.

Conservative political leaders have been vilified by their opponents for adopting a more conciliatory approach to Quebec. Liberal leaders, in particular Pierre Elliott Trudeau and Jean Chrétien, have proved to be intransigent to Quebec's claims and have been critical of other political leaders who have promulgated an accommodationist approach to securing Quebec's place in the Canadian federation. In fact, Liberal leaders have been systematic in their attempt to impose homogenizing policies on the entirety of the federation.[28] These policies have been opposed to the idea of recognizing the special status of a member state and to the recognition of Quebec as a distinct society. Eddie Goldenberg, Jean Chrétien's primary political adviser between 1993 and 2004, captures the Liberal approach and its distinctiveness from the Conservative project:

> The precise role of the federal government will remain at the center of these debates. Neo-conservatives will continue to argue for further restrictions on its powers, through strict interpretation of its constitutional rights, tax reductions, or by excessive fiscal transfers to the provinces; others, including myself, will continue to defend the idea that the federal government must ensure the well-being of the whole country and that it therefore requires important resources to fulfil its obligations, whether it be to fight against poverty, to improve health services, to support apprenticeships and higher education, to develop public infrastructure *or to respond to any other need of all Canadians.*[29]

This passage highlights the Liberal party's interventionist philosophy: the central government should not limit itself to its own jurisdiction, but must also impose its authority, policies, and social agenda when and where it is required. For the federal Liberal party this means embracing state intervention and subduing all other forms of nationalism and regionalism.[30] As mentioned in the previous section, the central government has a variety of tools at its disposal to implement this agenda, and this endangers the development of a federal culture in Canada.

In the case of the federal Liberals, the strategy consisted in using state interventionism to induce a strategy to feed centripetal forces in order to undermine all expressions of regionalism and nationalism. This way of capturing political dynamics overlooks the circuitous and off-stage ways in which the central government can impose, and has, its will on the member states. In fact, this understanding of strategies promotes a conceptualization of balance of power that vests all authority in the central government and dismisses the idea that, in a federation, sovereignty is shared between both orders of government.[31] Those who embrace the idea of containment/contentment also see the central government as the sole guarantor of individual rights and political stability. The central government has, in turn, promoted this idea and, in doing so, has proved to be generally unresponsive to legitimate claims making.

By denying the idea of shared sovereignty and accepting a central approach to politics, we deny the fact that Canada is in fact comprised of several *demoi* and not a single *demos*. The Supreme Court's secession reference (1998) highlights the existence of two national majorities in Canada: one in Quebec and one in the rest of Canada. It follows that

> so long as Quebec exercises its rights while respecting the rights of others, it may propose secession and seek to achieve it through negotiation. The negotiation process precipitated by a decision of a clear majority of the population of Quebec on a clear question to pursue secession would require the reconciliation of various rights and obligations by the representatives of two legitimate majorities, namely, the clear majority of the population of Quebec, and the clear majority of Canada as a whole, whatever that may be. There can be no suggestion that either of these majorities "trumps" the other. A political majority that does not act in accordance with the underlying constitutional principles we have identified puts at risk the legitimacy of the exercise of its rights.[32]

The secession reference points to the possibility of other methods of responding to claims making beyond the containment/contentment dyad. Should we not, then, do more than simply invoke the concept of balance of power, and instead envisage new scenarios that are sensitive to the legitimacy of collective actors? I turn to this issue in the second half of this chapter.

Two Conflicting Paradigms

There exists a rich and fast growing literature that focuses more and more on the concepts of "shared rule" and "self-rule." These concepts are also being taken more and more seriously in the study of federalism, especially by social scientists and political actors. In addition, there has been a marked interest in these concepts within international organizations called upon to settle conflicts in deeply divided societies.[33] In the Canadian context, the Meech Lake Accord, the Charlottetown Agreement, the two referenda in Quebec (1980, 1995), and the Quebec secession reference confirm an acceptance of the principle of shared rule. However, the central government has historically sought to promote a vision of the country resting on indivisible sovereignty. This push for the centralization of authority was on display during the negotiation of the Social Union Framework Agreement and during the Royal Commission on New Reproductive Technologies' consultations.[34] There are more examples of the central government's unwillingness to embrace a true federal culture[35] by enshrining the principle of shared rule. For one, health policy is under provincial jurisdiction yet the central government has persisted in imposing its will on this policy domain.

Within this context, the government of Quebec has, since the early 1960s, taken a stand against the central government's intrusion into its jurisdiction and has demanded a stricter interpretation and application of the division of powers. One way of guaranteeing this would be through the enshrinement of stricter rules of transparency and accountability, thus ensuring that the central government provides the member states with the opportunity to fulfil their constitutional obligations and allow them appropriate sources of revenue.

One should also note that claims making emanating from Atlantic and Western Canada is often focused on promoting greater representation within central institutions (the House of Commons and the Senate), in an attempt to gain a greater piece of the redistributive pie (equalization payments) or, as is the case for Alberta, in an attempt to revise contributions to federal income tax. In general, the least well-off provinces desire a greater degree of intervention from the central government (e.g., Maritime provinces, Manitoba and, until very recently, Saskatchewan), whereas the more prosperous provinces tend to see the central government as a threat to their autonomy.

Since 1867, with a few notable exceptions, political parties in Quebec have advanced the notion of governmental autonomy or, in other words, internal self-determination. The Parti Québécois has opted to promote the political project of self-determination both in its internal variant (i.e., good government) and in its external form (i.e., independence). However, most political parties have embraced the idea of internal self-determination. Over the last five decades, the Union Nationale, the Parti Québécois, the Quebec Liberal party, and the Action démocratique du Québec have adopted this stance. The Parti Québécois has on two occasions advanced the idea of external self-determination by holding referenda.

Nevertheless, political leaders in Quebec have occasionally sided with federal politicians to advance their claims. For example, the design and implementation of the Quebec Pension Plan in 1965 entailed an ideological convergence between Lester B. Pearson's federal Liberal government and Jean Lesage's Liberal administration in Quebec.[36] Following the Liberal party's defeat in Ottawa in 1984, the Parti Québécois, under the leadership of René Lévesque, opted to trust the Mulroney Conservative government. This led, as we have seen, to a

Quebec's representation within *la francophonie* and, subsequently, to the adoption of a new free-trade pact with the United States and of a new trade agreement covering the entirety of North America.

The new free-trade pact contributed to diversifying the Quebec market and to its unfettering from the Canadian economy. However, societal and political actors were divided on the long-term benefit of this pact. In fact, an important counter-mobilization emerged from the labour movement and from regions in Quebec that did not benefit from the new arrangement. The most common criticism of the pact pointed to the weakening of Quebec's internal autonomy as a result of a necessary convergence due to externally imposed economic rules. Facilitating Quebec's access to a much larger market also contributed to a decline, among the Anglo-Canadian left, in support for Quebec's claims for greater recognition; it provided an excuse for abandoning Quebec during the constitutional negotiations surrounding the Meech Lake Accord in the later 1980s and helped justify the disavowal of the enshrinement of distinct-society status during the negotiation of the Charlottetown Accord in 1992. Several key actors from the Canadian left took umbrage at Quebec's support for market liberalization, and this, in turn, led to a rupture between progressive forces in Quebec and similar forces in the rest of Canada.[37]

During Robert Bourassa's tenure as leader of the Quebec Liberal Party (1970–6 and 1985–94), a distinct openness to negotiation with the central government was present. This is evidenced by Bourassa's involvement in a series of proposed constitutional accords: the Victoria Agreement in 1971, the Meech Lake Accord 1987–90 and the Charlottetown Agreement 1992. The Meech Lake initiative would have provided Quebec with distinct society status; it would have reified Quebec's authority over immigration; it would have validated the importance of Quebec's distinct values by nominating three judges from the civil law tradition to the highest court in the land; it would have also restricted federal spending power in realms that were clearly under Quebec's jurisdiction and, finally, restored Quebec's historical right to a veto power. Although the accord received the support of the central government and of all of the first ministers during a first ministers conference held in Ottawa in June 1987, this support eroded when each legislative assembly was called upon to provide its formal approval of the accord and following claims by anti-Quebec political forces that the accord would entail the end of the Canadian nation as it was. The subsequent failure of the Meech Lake accord (and the Charlottetown

Agreement two years later) evidenced both the appeal and success of the containment strategy. Nonetheless, the failure of constitutional negotiations helped to further erode the bonds of trust between Quebec and the rest of Canada and, in turn, contributed to the emergence of le Bloc Québécois on the federal scene in August 1990, the election of the Parti Québécois in 1994, and by the referendum in 1995.[38]

The years following the failure of the 1995 referendum proved to be particularly difficult for Quebec; the central government attempted to impose its will, its way of doing things, and even its political leadership in realms that should have been, for all intents and purposes, under the sole jurisdiction of the member states. During the Liberal administrations of Jean Chrétien and Paul Martin, the central government pushed a centralizing agenda by restricting access to program financing and, in doing so, Ottawa used its spending power to dictate the rules of the game governing policies under provincial jurisdiction (health, higher education, transport and infrastructure, research and innovation, culture, leisure, etc.). Furthermore, a large sponsorship program was also initiated in an attempt to promote Canadian identity within Quebec's territory. These initiatives entailed massive squandering of public funds, leading to accusations of fraud and corruption within the Canadian government, and a number of political actors affiliated with the federal Liberal party were called to the witness stand to explain their actions during the Gomery inquiry[39] (otherwise known as the Commission of Inquiry into the Sponsorship Program and Advertising Activities).

Paradoxically, while Quebec has questioned aloud the central government's intrusion into its jurisdiction, other member states have welcomed it as an effective means to build new institutions. Thus, the adoption of the 1999 Social Union Framework Agreement was welcomed in many circles as it provided access to central government funding. Quebec found itself once again isolated as its core demands were overlooked during the federal-provincial negotiations. It would seem that other member states avoided siding with Quebec in order to avoid providing the Parti Québécois with political ammunition in a post-referendum context. The Canadian family had to present a common front; the slightest form of dissent would have been seen and presented as evidence of disloyalty to the idea of a united Canada.[40] The united front could not last forever, and eventually other regions, most notably Alberta and British Columbia, expressed their disagreement with the central government's position. It is within this context that Stephen Harper's Conservatives were able to take power in January 2006 under the banner of open federalism.[41]

The Conservative party sought to reverse the Liberal party's "closed federalism" by putting an end to squabbles between the central government and the member states and by allowing Quebec to play a more active role on the international scene. Although the Conservative party's ascent to power presaged new gains for Quebec, the Quebec Liberal party, under the leadership of Jean Charest from 2003 to 2012, was less than enthusiastic about engaging the central government.[42] To be sure, Benoît Pelletier, minister of Canadian intergovernmental affairs, made several important exploratory forays into this new environment. However, his recommendations and interventions were never truly embraced by the premier of Quebec. This response can be explained, in part, by the Charest government's reticence to heighten the expectations of the Quebec electorate, lest it fails and be held accountable by some form of political mobilization. Thus, under the Charest administration, the Quebec government removed itself from discussions of both internal and external self-determination. In brief, the strategy of containment seems to institute a culture of fear where political actors remain inactive in order to avoid backlashes both from within and without their territory.

Integration and Empowerment

Anglophone researchers in Canada focus primarily on the importance of central institutions as they relate to the construction of the Canadian federation. Within this context an important body of literature brings to light the distinction between intra-state federalism and inter-state federalism.[43]

This approach highlights an efficient way to counter sub-state national mobilization. In brief, it suggests emphasizing the importance of the centre (Canadian unity) instead of institutionalizing the federal principle (diversity). Federalism is thus presented as a means to initiate projects that value "coming together" as opposed to adopting mechanisms that lead to the "coming apart" of the polity; such an approach vests authority in the central government as the primary institution for maintaining political stability. This strategy, as opposed to containment and contentment, requires the integration of national and cultural minorities, the imposition of strong leadership from the centre and recognition that the central government is the ultimate protector of the federation.

Federal construction from the centre gives primacy to several institutions: the Canadian parliament, the Supreme Court, the Charter of Rights and Freedoms, pan-Canadian partisanship (i.e., brokerage politics), first ministers' conferences, royal commissions, recruitment policies for the federal public sector, and the Canadian Armed Forces. In sum, this strategy makes the centre the milieu par excellence of political competition and, concomitantly, affirms the second-class nature of the member states' governments. The notion of "coming apart" is used to deligitimize any political authority that does not emanate from the centre.

This approach goes against a principle of liberal thought that has long argued that conflict rather than consensus is necessary for governments to institute public policy that will lead to the advent of a truly democratic culture. Seen through this lens federations require conflict and tension in order to adopt better public policy.

Robert Dahl and Charles E. Lindblom have emphasized the importance of ideological pluralism (as opposed to the plurality of interests) as essential for the proper functioning of a democracy.[44] More recently, Dahl has argued that respect of cultural pluralism is also of vital importance for the deepening of democracy.[45] I fully embrace these ideas. Multinational polities must enshrine political engagement as a constant state of affairs and promote the importance of a federation's member states as active participants in the development of democratic practices. One of the best ways to counter political apathy is to promote active citizenship *at all levels of government*.

The central government has adopted other means to assert its influence: the federal Liberal party has promoted the centrality of Ottawa by institutionalizing regional ministries;[46] the central government has also oftentimes used its spending power to influence decision-making in areas where it has neither jurisdiction nor expertise. These manifestations of the integrationist strategy have nonetheless helped to reinforce sub-state national affirmation and, in turn, prevent the central government from achieving the desired integrationist outcome. On the flip side, a strategy of empowerment could help to develop a dialogue that, in the long run, could well lead to a convergence of political ideals.[47]

In Canada, the empowerment strategy has hardly been embraced, nor has inter-provincial rapprochement been truly encouraged. The

Council of the Federation, of which the central government is not a member, has struggled to take flight since its inception in 2003. Although some (e.g., the economist Thomas Courchene) see the council as an entity that is seeking citizen loyalty, others (such as the political scientist Alain Noël) see it as a key mechanism for redressing a power disequilibrium between orders of government and as a key tool for reversing Ottawa's centralizing imperative. Others (e.g., Benoît Pelletier) see it as the optimal way for provinces to develop a "creative politics" rather than simply being relegated to an "executive" politics dictated by the centre. Nevertheless, the council has not lived up to these ideals and, instead, has been a centre of inactivity, as member states rarely if ever reach consensus over political and social issues. Most recently, the council failed to act on the central government's decision to abandon the long-form census, despite the fact that the latter is essential to the good and equitable governance of the federation.[48]

Member states of the Canadian federation are subject to yet another form of internal colonization: they must defer to the central government's authority in the international arena in regards to their exclusive areas of expertise. In the 1960s, under the leadership of Jean Lesage, the Quebec government adopted a doctrine that would allow it to take its place in the international arena, albeit under the auspices of a clear division of powers between orders of government. This doctrine has manifested itself differently over the years. The Charest administration (2003–12) adopted a soft approach to international politics, focusing primarily on economic issues and avoiding, more or less, cultural and identity politics. In order to fully assume its national leadership, Quebec can and must develop a more ambitious foreign policy and assert itself on the international scene.[49]

Québécois and Canadians outside of Quebec have two distinct understandings of the division of powers and where sovereignty lies. Canadians outside of Quebec tend to see the central government as the repository of sovereignty, whereas Québécois tend to conceptualize power and sovereignty as shared between the central government and the member states. There are also those, however, who believe that sovereignty emanates from the member states and that the centre derives its legitimate authority from a compact devised in 1867, whereby the member states relinquished a certain degree of power in order to "come together" and rally around the federal ideal. We cannot therefore unilaterally endorse the central government's coercive power and sweep these competing perspectives under the rug.

Why do Québécois prefer the strategy of empowerment over the integrationist strategy? I would offer three explanations.

First, Québécois recognize the importance of undertaking and maintaining a national conversation within the community where their decision-making power will be felt instead of situating their debates in a territory under the control of another political community.[50] It is only within this context that the idea of Quebec as a nation, as a host society, as a context of choice, and as the repository of an intercultural demos takes its full meaning.

Second, the state cannot remain truly neutral given that it defends institutional arrangements that were designed to enshrine an imbalance of power and that invariably favour the national majority.[51] State institutions are protectors of the "coming together" approach rather than embodiments of an empowerment strategy; integrationist policies are, within this context, meant to institutionalize the national majority's hegemony; finally, interventionist politics, such as the Rowell-Sirois commission (1937–40), the enshrinement of the Charter of Rights and Freedoms of 1982, and the adoption of a national health policy (1982), as well as the Canadian Social Union (1999), have as a primary goal the entrenchment of a common pan-Canadian identity.

Members of the national majority often suggest that an integrationist approach is one that members of national minorities themselves should desire. In Canada – a multinational country if there ever was one – this view suggests that the central government can speak on behalf of a unified Canadian people, and a universally applied charter. Politicians like Paul Martin, in the 2006 federal election, have gone so far as to challenge the notwithstanding clause on the grounds that it threatens individual rights and freedoms. Is it not true, however, that the notwithstanding clause was intended to provide all members of the minority nations with a degree of parliamentary sovereignty within the wider scope and operation of Canadian institutions?[52] It should be kept in mind that the notwithstanding clause was included in the Canadian constitution precisely because it provides Quebec with some protection from the possibility that the anglophone provinces use Canada's majoritarian central institutions against Quebec. Why has there been an attack on those who wish to protect the sovereignty of minority nations?

Third, Québécois are highly suspicious of multilateral political arrangements; they see within these arrangements the threat of "minoritizing" a people. They have a right to worry: over the last three decades, Quebec has been politically isolated during the repatriation of the constitution, during the negotiation of the Meech Lake Accord, during the Charlottetown discussions, and at the moment of the adoption of the Social Union Framework Agreement. Quebec has responded to these multilateral arrangements in two ways: by playing an active role in the Council of the Federation[53] and by undertaking bilateral negotiations with the central government. The first response was met by a divide-and-conquer strategy whereby the central government negotiated individual equalization-payment agreements with each member state. The second response (bilateralism) has been met with vocal opposition by other members of the Council of the Federation. As a result, Quebec has remained relatively silent on this front since 2003. In brief, there is much to be done in order to activate and enshrine new arenas of legitimate authority.

✌︎

The work of Isaiah Berlin, which served as an inspiration for this chapter, can help to shed new light on issues of liberty and self-determination, in both its external and internal variations. It behoves us now to extend this framework by focusing on national communities rather than individuals[54] and by drawing a conceptual distinction between negative and positive autonomy. It is here that we find a happy marriage between comparative politics and political theory. The conceptual distinction between negative and positive autonomy has important ramifications for the subject of political relations between minority and majority nations. The distinction, proposed by Berlin, helps counter paternalistic arguments used by supporters of unitary states (like today's unionists in Scotland) who believe that that undivided sovereignty should exist at the centre, with its power to coerce or compel. Viewing power relations in this way is outdated and fails to give proper respect to the various communities from which the centre's political authority stems.

Supporters of integration, instead of assimilation, indeed contribute to the flourishing of liberalism in society. In addition, it is important to take matters one step further by supporting national communities against misrecognition[55] and disempowerment.[56] To this end, it is critical that we question political authority in another way, by considering the balance of power and the legitimacy of all political actors within the shared multinational state. Any attack on negative autonomy (*freedom from*) or positive autonomy (*freedom to*) must be denounced if we are to provide members of national minorities with a context of choice that meets liberalism's standards. Autonomy for national communities thus understood should not be seen as limiting some external authority (e.g., the state), but as a form of emancipation from the notion of contentment mentioned earlier.

Social scientists will have their hands full trying to consider the full policy implications of this new approach to constitutionalism.[57] For instance, difficult questions must be answered like: how do we entrench such a notion of autonomy? Part of the answer has been provided in the preceding chapters. Multinational states must be open to recognizing claims making rooted in historical continuity. We must also promote intra-national dialogue and respect within shared institutions. As Tully suggests, we must put an end to imperialist practices and recognize informal constitutions.[58] To get there, an unavoidable obligation would be to pursue the democratic conversation while being aware of the existence of relationships of unequal political force.

Minority nations in both Quebec and Catalonia face serious challenges with respect to the majority nations with which they share a state. It is imperative that all members embrace their responsibilities and commit themselves to long-term solutions based on a dialogical approach that acknowledges and accepts the tension between power imbalances and minority nation-building projects.[59] This makes it possible to promote a broader, pluralistic, and inclusive vision for multinational federations. In other words, an unavoidable political obligation remains among constituent national communities to continue a democratic conversation that acknowledges power imbalances and their ongoing effects – particularly on minority nations.

5 Towards Multinational Federalism: Moving beyond the Integration-Accommodation Dyad

At the moment, might lies with the majority and right with the minority. Mutual recognition must rebalance the relationship, with both power and legitimacy finding a new equilibrium.

Michael Ignatieff[1]

Several models have been developed in order to respond to the needs of political communities. Consociationalism, federalism, and territorial and cultural autonomy are among the main institutional arrangements that are proposed for accommodating national pluralism.[2] In this chapter, I highlight the reasons why territorial autonomy is currently experiencing some significant setbacks in the Western world and making no real progress elsewhere.[3] I also want to propose a way out of this predicament. First of all, I will explore the contradictory way in which governments and international organizations have blown both hot and cold with respect to the treatment of national diversity; those who were previously inclined to support territorial autonomy as a way of managing national diversity have gradually retreated from this position and now encourage the containment or even outright assimilation of national diversity. It is difficult to imagine the two latter approaches (containment and assimilation) as providing a basis for trust among communities in contexts where minority nations are threatened by institutionalized domination. Second, I will turn to the major debate in political science concerning rival strategies for ensuring the stability of existing states. On one side of this debate there are those who support the institutional accommodation of national minorities; on the other side there are those who argue that national minorities ought to be integrated within a common identity. As I will explain, both sides of this debate make hierarchical assumptions about the relationship between national majorities and minorities, tending to see national pluralism as a "problem" to be managed by the state. I argue instead that we need to go beyond the integration-accommodation dyad and envision more egalitarian possibilities that are based on the empowerment of national communities rather than the mere recognition and accommodation of difference. To that end, I argue that multinational federalism offers a third alternative, one in which majorities and minorities can relate to one another on the basis of equal partnership and both types of communities are properly equipped to address pressing social and economic needs.

States Facing National Diversity: Between Territorial Autonomy and Containment

Beginning in 1989–90, and under the approving eye of Western countries, a number of new states emerged following the collapse of communism and the break-up of the Soviet Union. These new states rapidly received the benediction of major Western powers and international organizations that saw an opportunity to advance democracy – and capitalism too of course – across vast territories that had until then been difficult to access. This was the beginning of a wave of sympathy and support for those national minorities which had previously lived under Soviet domination. Since then, however, the approach of the international community has been inconsistent. Will Kymlicka[4] has plotted the contradictory positions adopted by international organizations with respect to the recognition of the rights of national minorities over the last two decades, has looked at the situation of Aboriginal communities in the Americas and national minorities in Europe, and has also explored the difficulties in transplanting liberal multiculturalism to Africa and Asia. Kymlicka[5] notes that, in recent years, international organizations, including the United Nations, the Organization for Security and Cooperation in Europe (OSCE), and the Council of Europe, have taken much less conciliatory and often contradictory positions with respect to national minorities. These organizations seem to be increasingly in favour of national integration policies instead of the accommodation policies for which they were the standard-bearers only a few years earlier.

However, over the last two decades the growing number of new states on the political chessboard has caused an increasing discomfort among the major powers and international organizations. The major powers, which are sometimes also under pressure domestically from sub-state nationalism or minority nationalism, often adopt a common stand against the recognition or promotion of national diversity in established states. At the very most, the major powers are ready to recognize the right to domestic self-determination of Aboriginal peoples – which proves in the end to have few consequences – but they have been generally deaf to the right to self-determination of national minorities, whether at home or abroad.

This change in priorities at the very heart of international institutions has led some national minorities to describe themselves as indigenous groups in an effort to obtain benefits to which they would not otherwise have access. Kymlicka provides a number of examples of this kind of identification shift, such as that of Berber tribes in Algeria and the Arabic-speaking population in the Ahwaz region of Iran. Today, leaders of other minority groups, such as the Tatars in Crimea, Gypsies, Kurds, Palestinians, Chechens, and Tibetans, are also considering adopting a similar strategy.

Thus, with respect to the rights of national minorities, it seems that the dynamic has been reversed since the fall of the Berlin Wall and the collapse of communism. This change in attitude runs against the norms that were previously endorsed by the international community. The Copenhagen Declaration, issued in June 1990 at the Conference on Security and Cooperation in Europe, establishes the principle of territorial autonomy for national minorities and recognizes in paragraph 35 that the participating OSCE states "will respect the right of persons belonging to national minorities to effective participation in public affairs, including participation in the affairs relating to the protection and promotion of the identity of such minorities."[6] Moreover, the participating states agreed to set up a series of positive action measures in favour of national minorities, while also fighting against all forms of discrimination on their territories. Similarly, paragraph 15 of the Council of Europe's 1994 Framework Convention on the Protection of National Minorities requires that the signatories "shall create the conditions necessary for the effective participation of persons belonging to national minorities in cultural, social and economic life and in public affairs, in particular those affecting them."[7]

We could have expected then that the OSCE would fight tooth and nail for the institution of a system favourable to national minorities, especially since in both of the documents cited above there is specific recognition of rights of national minorities that have to be respected by majority nations.

Things have changed significantly over the last decade, however, and major backpedalling seems to be going on in international organizations. For one thing, the flow of official texts supporting territorial autonomy has dried up. Specific reference was not made to the principle of territorial autonomy for national minorities in subsequent OSCE declarations at the Hague in 1996, Oslo in 1998, and Lund in 1999. At the Hague the issue was minorities' rights to education. At Oslo the issue was minorities' linguistic rights. There has also been much less focus on national minorities as such, and more focus on minorities differentiated according to culture, sex, politics, and ethnic origin. In effect, an "identity approach," rather than one based on the affirmation of national diversity, is in vogue. Moreover, international players are trying to persuade stakeholders that what is important is not so much governmental autonomy, but rather political participation on the part of minorities and good governance.[8] The consequences of this sea change are potentially grave for the plight of national minorities.[9]

What is perhaps even more striking is that the Venice commission (an advisory committee to the Council of Europe on constitutional matters) does not recognize a right to external self-determination or any right to domestic self-determination in its 1996 opinion on the rights of national minorities. Indeed, if we look at the Venice commission's opinion on the interpretation of the Draft Protocol of the European Convention on Human Rights appended to recommendation 1201 of the Parliamentary Assembly (1993), it is clear that

> [s]tates seem in fact to be afraid that the right to have appropriate local or autonomous administrations, combined with the right to transfrontier contacts (Article 10 of the draft protocol), may promote secessionist tendencies. Even those States which, while adhering to the principle of unity have granted a large degree of regional autonomy hesitate to accept binding international instruments on the right of minorities to autonomy.[10]

This simply amounts to a slippery-slope argument. Opponents of the right to territorial autonomy fear that it is too easy to go from cultural autonomy to administrative autonomy, and then to secession.[11] According to the Venice commission's opinion, we have to avoid giving any foothold to national minorities; otherwise they will mobilize citizens around nationalistic claims. In short, the primary objective is to make independence as difficult as possible. Thus, given the prevailing suspicion, national minorities must overcome more obstacles than ever.

To be sure, there are some positive signs. Specialists in international law are now relatively open to the recognition of Aboriginal peoples' right to internal self-determination. Indeed, a broad consensus has been built regarding this point. Yet, these same specialists, who are generally recognize the full enjoyment of basic individual freedoms for members of minority nations through individualistic bills of rights, are much less open when it comes to recognizing the right of minority nations to have full territorial autonomy. The argument is that territorial autonomy is possible only if minority nations in no way seek to exercise their right to self-determination.

Instead of putting up new barriers, should we not, in Daniel Innerarity's words, try to develop a "hospitality ethic" so that the different member nations living within a multinational state can fully flourish? The current situation prevailing, for instance, in Spain requires that political and social players be uncommonly imaginative; political models that respect national diversity must be devised; institutions must be reimagined on a more democratic and equitable basis.

Integration, Accommodation, and Empowerment

Meanwhile, scholars in the disciplines of political science, philosophy, and law have also been engaged in a major debate about the best way to manage cultural and national diversity. Running through this debate is what John McGarry, Brendan O'Leary, and Richard Simeon have identified as an "integration-accommodation continuum," and they have joined with those who promote various forms of accommodation for national minorities. McGarry, O'Leary, and Simeon are supportive of claims from national minorities in existing states, so long as minorities comply with established democratic practices and do not undermine/challenge the stability of existing regimes. This position is very different from that of other researchers, who argue that accommodation practices in terms of positive action for minorities, as well as in terms of education and religious rights can, in Sujit Choudhry's words, "entrench, perpetuate and exacerbate the very divisions they are designed to manage."[12]

Arend Lijphart, the pioneer of the study of "consociational" democracies, warns us of the dangers of denying the existence of national minorities or of trying to shift their allegiance to, for example, a broader political community or majority nation. According to Lijphart:

> Although the replacement of segmental loyalties by a common national allegiance appears to be a logical answer to the problems posed by a plural society, it is extremely dangerous to attempt it. Because of the tenacity of primordial loyalties, any effort to eradicate them not only is quite unlikely to succeed, especially in the short run, but may well be counterproductive and may stimulate segmental cohesion and intersegmental violence rather than national cohesion.[13]

There are many ways of managing conflicts, but not all respect democratic traditions. As Guy Laforest argues, prudence is needed today more than ever.[14]

But the use of the integration-accommodation dyad leads to an impasse and, as I posit, simply soothes the consciences of majority nations. In fact, it is one and the same dynamic. The integration-accommodation dyad preserves hierarchical power relations. A majority nation might employ integration policies in cases where the minority nations are dispersed, but employ more or less ambitious accommodation policies when minority nations are concentrated and could put up political resistance. Yet, the intention remains the same: the perpetuation of power relationships that are unfavourable to minority nations, and this intention feeds minority nations' distrust of dominant groups.[15]

Consider Brendan O'Leary's penetrating text[16] on the "federal staatsvolk." O'Leary argues that the survival of democratic federations depends on there being a "staatsvolk," in other words, a nation or ethnic group that can demographically and electorally dominate the other communities. O'Leary states that the minimum population threshold for a staatsvolk is 50 per cent, and that the more self-confidence the majority nation has, the more able it will be to make concessions to minority nations. Concessions will in turn raise the level of comfort of minority nations within a given state.

Indeed, accommodation mechanisms such as territorial autonomy and territorial-cultural autonomy have been adopted in a number of multinational states. Generally, however, the tendency is towards the consolidation of political control[17] and institutionalized domination by the majority nation[18] rather than the empowerment of minority nations. Concessions have been permitted, so long as they do not open the way to national independence. At the most, territorial cultural autonomy is seen as a legitimate form of governance, but not as a means for minority nations concentrated in specific territories to achieve full emancipation.

In a manner similar to the approach underlying the territorial cultural autonomy model – which provides no guarantees of peoples' rights to decide freely for themselves – Jim Tully defends a diversity-recognition policy. Tully sees this as a practical and even ideal way of securing the constitutional allegiance of national minorities in existing nation states without challenging the legitimacy of those states.[19]

It should be noted that even for authors who are sensitive to issues arising out of deep diversity, the issue of diversity in the form of more than one nation is still a considerable challenge. In this sense, arguments such as O'Leary's and even Tully's are not much consolation to minority nations. Members of minority nations are less interested in being accommodated by the majority group – though such things can lead to some advances – than in establishing a real "equal-to-equal" partnership. The idea is not to be in the position of begging for dispensations, but to be a negotiator aiming to achieve an agreed partnership based on a set of principles that respect community pluralism, ideological pluralism, and (why not) even legal pluralism. What we should be aiming at today then is to identify options that might reverse existing systems of domination, a goal which receives only lip service from the integration and accommodation schools of thought. To this end, we have to look beyond the mere recognition or accommodation of difference – though this is an essential point of departure – to the idea of empowerment. Such an approach would seek to enable both majority and minority nations to acquire the tools needed for their full flourishing as communities. It is here that multinational federalism may yet hold its greatest potential.

Multinational Federalism as an Empowering Force for National Minorities

To be sure, the status quo approach endorsed by the international community and the accommodationist school might be capable of satisfying some national groups. However, these approaches do not seem to provide an adequate answer to the demands for emancipation that are specific to minority nations that are highly developed in terms of identity and in terms of social, political, and institutional distinctiveness. Nations like Quebec, Scotland, and Catalonia (and a number of other minority nations in Western states) are members of a select group of nations that might aspire to acquire a new status among nation states. But this new status would require that majority nations rethink state institutions so as to give flesh to the multinational foundations on which the legitimacy of those states is based.[20]

In an article entitled "From Dominance to Partnership,"[21] Michael Burgess invites political players and specialists of federalism to abandon the concept of domination and instead endorse the idea of partnerships among political communities. Burgess argues that minority nations should be recognized as having a right to domestic self-determination, while central governments could try to promote an encompassing "political nationality" that would accommodate both the majority nation and minority nations in the context of multinational federalism.

Indeed, a number of partnership systems have been considered by political leaders in Quebec over the last fifty years. For example, there was the "associated states" arrangement proposed by the Parti Québécois under the reign of René Lévesque. There was also the "associated sovereign states" concept (i.e., the "Brussels question") evoked by Robert Bourassa. Finally, there was the "sovereignty-partnership" concept advanced by Jacques Parizeau and Lucien Bouchard during the October 1995 referendum campaign. However, these systems were all proposed as *alternatives* to federalism.

It is well known of course that Canadian federalism does not generally get very good press in Quebec. There are a number of reasons for this, but it is mainly because in its implementation Canadian federalism has often been synonymous with the reproduction of power relations that are unfavourable to the Quebec nation.[22] In 2006, however, a number of colleagues and I published *Le fédéralisme canadien contemporain*[23] in which we showed that there is a school of federalist thought specific to Quebec. Members of the school challenge the territorial vision of Canadian federalism and propose a multinational reading of federalism. Today there is a wealth of writing on multinational federalism in Canada, but there has been a heavy tendency among English-Canadian authors to give precedence to a purely territorial interpretation. This choice has consequences. We have only to think about the importance of the Supreme Court of Canada's *Reference re the Secession of Quebec*. In Canada, there has been an effort to impose a hierarchical vision of federalism by replacing the notion of *orders* of government with that of *levels* of government.

But federalism does not have to be imperialistic, hierarchical or authoritarian. Federalism can also institutionalize equal, respectful power relationships among national communities, and enable stakeholders to focus on relations of non-domination among different orders of government. Federalism also makes it possible to think about sovereignty as shared between two orders of government without a hierarchy being imposed from above. As I have shown in a recent book entitled *The Case for Multinational Federalism*, federalism can have clear advantages for national political communities so long as the central power respects the autonomy of member states and does not try to appropriate powers that are not in its jurisdiction by invoking the "national interest" at the expense of any other basis for political legitimacy. I do not think that such a "control policy," to borrow Lustik's concept, can itself be legitimate in any way. The objective should be to find a healthy balance between different political communities, such that members of minority nations can realize possibilities that are comparable to those enjoyed by members of majority nations. This quest for balance would renew trust between communities, as well as empower minority nations to achieve greater emancipation on the cultural, economic, institutional, legal, social, and political levels. Such an empowerment policy would allow Quebec, like Scotland and Catalonia, for example, to establish effective policies for receiving and integrating immigrants,[24] as well as giving them the essential tools for making their citizenship policies more coherent and grounded.

⚬⚭⚬

In *The Case for Multinational Federalism* I looked at just how difficult it has been to establish a school of diversity in Canada and Spain, even though these countries are multinational in nature. This is due in part to power relations in Spain that are unfavourable to historic nations, and to an imperial relationship in Canada with Quebec that has been maintained by central institutions since the very beginning of Confederation. I have tried to explore further this issue here by looking at the contributions of both international institutions and researchers in the debate about how national communities are to get along together.

As we have seen from the analysis of territorial autonomy and the status of national minorities in existing states, the answers have varied, but since 1990, opposition to territorial claims has been clearer. Legal theorist Francesco Palermo[25] even goes so far as to argue that national minorities still do not have a recognized right to autonomy and that the exercise of that right varies depending on the whims of the existing nation state. When the approach has gone beyond the pure and simple containment of minority nations, dispensations have generally been limited to territorial autonomy.

Does the treatment of minority nations have to be as such, and which principles ought we to invoke in order to build a better scenario? Below, I sketch four such principles that help elucidate this issue:

- The first principle is the right to self-determination of peoples, which is usually understood in opposition to the principle of territorial integrity;[26]
- The second principle is that of the legitimacy of recognition claims, which are compared with the legality of empowerment strategies;[27]
- The third principle consists in seeking cultural preservation of national minorities and a corresponding focus on the capacity for survival and integration;[28]
- The fourth principle consists in placing the accent on concrete/real equality rather than on formal equality (Charter of Rights).

These are the kinds of normative principles that might inspire scenarios that are more supportive of the claims of national minorities inside or outside existing states, in contrast to the generally unsympathetic attitude of international organizations. It is clear that the latter are trying to keep things calm and maintain the status quo, especially with respect to the territorial integrity of existing states. The imperatives of institutional stability are almost always defended by the High Commissioner on National Minorities. The commissioner's support for recognition of Crimea's territorial autonomy in the Ukraine in the early 1990s is a major exception to this rule.[29] Another more recent example is the case of Kosovo, which received the blessing of the United States. In short and to conclude, it is important to go further in our reflection on the autonomy of national minorities by drawing upon the work of comparativists, legal theorists, and political philosophers alike. This undertaking is essential for maintaining good relations among national communities while at the same time guaranteeing a democratic future for all citizens.

6 Rethinking Intercommunal Relations in Canada

The question is still if there are some kind of federal agreements capable of articulating states with complex territorial and national identities, from a liberal perspective of *political recognition*. This is currently one of the most important challenges of federalism.

Ferran Requejo[1]

Solutions for reconciling different communities often vary in accordance to power relations, as well as economic and political interests. With respect to political tensions between Quebec and Canada, we find several distinguished authors who have contributed to the present debate. Of note, among others, are the reflections of Roger Gibbins, Jane Jenson, Will Kymlicka, Guy Laforest, Kenneth McRoberts, Alain Noël, and Benoît Pelletier. In an edited volume by François Rocher and David Schneiderman, *Beyond the Impasse, Towards Reconcilation,*[2] almost all options for dealing with Quebec–Canada tensions were taken into consideration except for the idea of secession, which was excluded at the very outset as a possible outcome. I will now review briefly some key contributions to the volume. Philosopher Will Kymlicka discusses the coexistence of territorial federalism and multinational federalism in complex states and even goes as far as stating, in the Canadian case, "the need to explicitly recognize our multinational character, if we expect to obtain the willing participation of these cultural minorities in a new partnership."[3] Meanwhile, jurist David Schneiderman discusses openly the possibility of having different legal systems coexisting within the same state, going as far as envisaging for Canada "a regime of legal pluralism with multiple charters of rights ... These charters and autonomous regimes are considered structurally compatible and entitled to status as constitutional law."[4] The reading of Schneiderman is all the more important as it invites a reflection on the foundation of pactism.

For her part, political scientist Jane Jenson specifies that "any movement toward partnership [between Canada and Quebec], must take into account the following fact: Two distinct societies are housed within a single country, and each has its own citizenship regime."[5] This does not mean that the two communities do not share certain values, but rather that they diverge significantly in the way in which they understand the foundations of the state and the relationship between state, civil society, and the market.

Finally, political theorist Guy Laforest, who notes an important mistrust and imbalance in prevailing political forces, invites political leaders to rethink the Canadian federation on a new basis that is more egalitarian and in tune with deep diversity. Also, political leaders are invited to determine in a free and open manner "the degree of sovereignty to be enjoyed by the various political communities, both in the federal context and within the confederational framework of the partnership Union"[6] in their attempts to overcome the Canadian impasse. As a result, each of these authors, by mining their field of expertise, invites political actors to take claims made by Quebec seriously and, by extension, similar claims expressed by minority nations in other federal states or those in the process of federalization, lest issues at stake ultimately remain unresolved.

This work, *Beyond the Impasse, Towards Reconciliation*, remains a highly relevant contribution today, especially for those societies in the midst of tensions related to their identity, as are many minority nations. The cases of Catalonia, Scotland, Greenland, and Quebec immediately come to mind. We must now rethink the means of achieving reconciliation, and towards this end I organize this chapter in the following three sections. First, there is a need to return to the sources of pactism in order to find relevant lessons for pluralist societies that are evolving into complex states. In the second section, I stress how practices specific to federalism may show us the way towards inter-communal rapprochement. And in the third, I explore the notion of "treaty federalism" as an expression of the fusion of different federal practices and pactism.

Pactism

Experts on federalism are generally quite familiar with the notion of pacts. In fact, the concept of federalism originated from the latin *foedus*, which means a covenant or pact. It is, furthermore, what led John Kincaid, who is continuing Daniel Elazar's work, to articulate that

> a covenant signifies a binding partnership among co-equals in which the parties to the covenant retain their individual identity and integrity while creating a new entity, such as a family or a body politic, that has its own identity and integrity as well. A covenant also signifies a morally binding commitment in which the partners behave toward each other in accord with the spirit of the law rather than merely the letter of the law. Thus, the binding agreement is more than a contract. A covenant commits the parties to an enduring, even perpetual, relationship and to an obligation to cooperate to achieve the ends of the agreement and to resolve peacefully the conflicts that invariably arise in every relationship.[7]

These pacts are both real and imagined. As Kincaid mentions, pacts go well beyond contracts since, while constituting a principle of organization, they presume good faith of the actors in their will to respect the expectations of others. It is essential to update these pacts, since communities (which they were designed to serve use them as a reference) evolve and may want to reconsider earlier agreements in order to face unexpected challenges. This is precisely what the authors of *Beyond the Impasse* endeavour to address in the Canadian case.

In this chapter, I seek to further our understanding of the subject by re-examining the foundation of the pact, while bearing in mind the unilateral repatriation of the Constitution Act, 1982, and attempts at constitutional revision which occurred thereafter.[8]

The notion of pactism can trace its origins to the Middle Ages. It involves the recognition of a pact between communities under the same political body which then becomes a new political authority. Political pactism puts forth "a definition of the balance of power between the sovereign and the various communities which represent the people, the Cortès, Corts or States. It is the battlefield on which the fight for the administration of justice and the creation of a fiscal administration, takes place."[9] Barraqué recalls that "the political existence of the country precedes that of the sovereign. The legitimacy of the sovereign is assured only insofar as it upholds its commitment to respect the pact, and that this commitment is, indeed, adhered to."[10] This way of conceiving things led to the concept of loyalty, which is the foundation of pactism. When loyalty towards customs and established practices was lacking, the people would become free from their obligations and the monarch would lose all legitimacy.

Of course, pactism brings together political and social actors of different strengths and, thus, makes respect for the pact a question of honour and mutual trust. Francesc Eiximenis (1330–1409), a Catalan, is perhaps the person who most contributed to its conceptualization. Eiximenis states that "if the prince does not observe the pacts without good reason, it is then clear that he must be deposed, if not, he has no right to retain sovereignty, like a tyrant."[11] To act in such a way would jeopardize the sense of togetherness and seriously impoverish political and social life.

In the current context, though the parliaments of Catalonia and Spain have both looked favourably upon the new autonomous status approved by the Catalan nation in a 2006 referendum, Catalan thinkers encourage the various actors involved to reappropriate the lessons of Eixemenis in order to restore the bond between Catalans and the central state. There is a need to rally around the principles identified by Eiximenis: good-faith negotiations, respect for social diversity, law, and justice as sources of sovereignty, the essential place of virtue in political life, and the promotion of harmony. Furthermore, one will find that centuries later, these same concepts are at the heart of the political ideals of the French enlightenment[12] and, subsequently, in the writings of the Scottish enlightenment, especially those of David Hume and Adam Ferguson.[13]

To rethink the means of reconciliation in a context of national diversity also requires the presence of an authentic federal culture in which it will be possible for nations, on the basis of a founding pact, to imagine and build a common future.

Establishing and Promoting a Federal Culture

Curiously, the majority of experts on federalism have given the concept of "federal culture" little attention. Those experts have shown themselves to be much more interested in dealing with institutional questions (i.e., federations), as opposed to normative issues pertaining to the setting up and renewal of federal structures.

There are, however, some important studies related to the notion of a federal spirit. For example, the analysis of Rufus Davis and the subject of his work *The Federal Principle: A Journey through Time in Quest of Meaning*.[14] Davis speaks at great length about the concept of the "covenant," of the bonds of reciprocity between the partners and of the obligation to come to agreements negotiated in good faith. Michael Burgess expands this even further than Davis, by touching on the moral and normative underpinnings of federal arrangements. Burgess identifies essential values in terms of concretizing the pact as a result of the presence of a federal culture: a culture that would be founded on the principles of mutual respect, recognition, dignity, tolerance, reciprocity and integrity.[15]

One should note that there is a strong bias in the studies of federalism in favour of American federalism as a model to be emulated. However, the American model does not take into account social diversity and does not recognize the needs of national communities. Miquel Caminal, as well as Ferran Requejo, confirm the overemphasis of the American model in the existing literature on federalism and discuss the difficulties for those subscribing to other federal traditions[16] when they propose different ways of managing national diversity and alternative means to enshrining a federal culture in political institutions.

There are occasional references to the federal ideal in the work of Ivo Duchacek, Daniel Elazar, and, more recently, Dimitrios Karmis, but, apart from these exceptions,[17] very few authors feel the need to look further into the notion of federal pluralism or the federal culture that ought to underpin it.[18] Daniel Elazar, in *Exploring Federalism*, notes that to have success, federal countries must not only be engaged in a federal way of thinking, but must also have a strong federal tradition in order to make use of the principles underlying it.[19]

In the wake of Elazar's work, it is necessary to highlight the important contribution of Samuel LaSelva to our understanding of the normative basis underlying federalism.[20] His work has had a major impact in recent years on the study of federalism and has contributed to the expansion of the scope of research, to the extent that it now goes beyond the traditional study related to constitutional and legal arrangements.[21]

It is also necessary to highlight Karmis's work regarding the concept of "pluralist federalism." Whereas his predecessors spoke mainly about federal culture, the pluralist federal model establishes "cultural diversity as a good that must be recognized," and argues that "the recognition of a federal status for members of territorialized communities entails, on a moral and sociological level, a broader concern with cultural recognition, including the recognition of minorities created by the federal structure itself." Furthermore, pluralist federalism entails the acceptance of "new struggles for recognition" such as belonging to a "never-ending process" of identity assertion.[22] The recognition of these various elements would result in a pact that could be renewed on a regular basis for as long as it endures, as it will be nurtured by an emancipating federal culture.

The idea of seeking to instil a federal culture for countries with national diversity is not a new one. Experts in comparative federalism, for example Ronald Watts and Michael Burgess, saw therein an essential element, along with the stability of the political regime. We should also note that Watts is one of the most consulted experts by leaders of countries with significant intercommunal tensions. In recent years, Watts has been asked to give opinions on the situations in India, Ethiopia, South Africa, and Eastern Europe. On each occasion, he insisted on emphasizing the advantages of a federal culture for states in search of solutions based on negotiations and democracy,[23] without which the energies invested in reforms would be in vain.

Watts reminds us that it is essential for a state that is multinational, and that is aspiring to have a promising future, to build a system on a solid basis of values that are compatible with a federal culture. In short, it is important for the national groups involved to show proof of compromise, tolerance, and respect for diversity, and to maintain and strengthen bonds based on trust between partners, while adhering to an ensemble of shared values. These ideas are not new; they are, however, too often neglected by political actors in a position of power dominance. The latter usually seek to impose their own way of doing things on national groups that are in the minority. The establishment of pluralist federalism is that much more important when it allows for the abandonment of this monolithic vision, which has so often, since the very creation of nation states, strained relations between the dominant nation and minority nations.[24]

Over the course of the last decade, Michael Burgess has become one of the foremost experts on federalism and has made the largest contribution to its study. Burgess's innovation is to compare countries that are founded upon federal culture in its most advanced form (Switzerland), at the intermediate level (Canada), and at its weakest level (Nigeria). It is in comparing those that he is able to identify the fundamentals of the "federal condition." It is worth quoting Burgess extensively, given the value of his analysis and its importance for the understanding of federal culture:

> The federal polity is founded on certain shared assumptions, values, beliefs and interests that together presuppose the politics of recognition, cooperation, compromise and accommodation. This is because the polity is rooted in notions of human dignity, toleration, respect, reciprocity, and consent. And since the federal idea is predicated upon difference and

diversity, … its very conception presupposes a particular orientation in politics … It is, in short, a prescription, a recommendation, a normative empirical approach to managing conflicts in societies where there are pronounced levels of difference and diversity having political salience.[25]

The thought processes of these Canadian and British colleagues, Watts and Burgess, make them extremely well equipped, as researchers, to face the struggles in several countries to identify the means for an honourable exit from their crises. The cases are too numerous to mention here, but among those that are particularly noteworthy are Ethiopia, Iraq, Malaysia, Nigeria, Sudan, and, even in the heart of the European Union, Belgium and Spain. The latter, having long neglected their existential crises, are increasingly embroiled in systemic tensions and constantly postpone the future establishment of an authentically pluralist federalism.[26]

In an important work published in 2002,[27] Raoul Blindenbacher and Ronald Watts attempted to test certain hypotheses with the aim of measuring the presence of a federal culture in Canada. Once the characteristics inherent in a federal community have been identified (i.e., two orders of government, negotiated division of powers, representation of members states within the central institutions, constitutional amendments according to established standards based on consent, independent constitutional courts to settle disputes, mechanisms of coordination, cooperation, and co-decision), the authors assess whether there is a federal culture or not in a given country. To this end, they identify five key aspects (see below) underlying the political culture, which were subsequently revisited by Jean-François Caron, Guy Laforest, and Catherine Vallières-Roland in *Contemporary Canadian Federalism*.[28] Those authors added a sixth element to the original set of variables. Elements necessary for the presence of a federal culture are:

1. A strong disposition by the constituent entities of the federal regime to democratize procedures;
2. Non-centralization as a working principle expressed through multiple centres of political decision-making;
3. Open bargaining processes;
4. The existence of counterweights (checks and balances) to avoid the concentration of political power;
5. A respect for constitutionalism and the rule of law;
6. Adaptability of the constitutional framework and flexibility of institutional mechanisms.[29]

The presence of these elements attests to the existence of a true federal culture in a democratic context. In short, to the extent that these elements can be found, it will be possible to engender feelings of tolerance of and respect for diversity based on compromise and, thus, strengthen relations between communities. In such a context, it can be presumed that national communities, interacting on a regular basis, will have the necessary intrinsic qualities that enable responsible management of national diversity, along with revitalization of the foundations of the federal arrangements.

This brief discussion of a federal culture allows us to make some association with a heritage based on a tradition of pactism. The presence of these two elements (pactism tradition, federal culture) is essential to the success of the policies of intercommunal reconciliation in democratic federal states.[30] The loyalty of national communities to the federal state will be proportional to their recognition and their empowerment, whereas, I would argue, the absence of recognition of national diversity along with a division of powers that favours the central government will have the opposite effect. Support of these same national communities for the agenda of the central government will be proportional to the willingness of the latter to support the claims made by member states in their exclusive jurisdictions. One could express this through the principles of reciprocity and mutual respect.

To the extent that these principles are emulated, it will be possible to imagine the bringing together of these communities, and even a communal coexistence. In the next section, I will more explicitly delve into the study of the optimal way of managing diversity in the context of multinational federalism, that is to say, "conventional constitutionalism" or "treaty federalism."

Treaty Federalism

In the two preceding sections, I explored the potential reconciling effects of pactism for countries experiencing tensions, while, at the same time, assessing the importance of this institution for nurturing a federal culture, characterized by national diversity, for democratic states. Two dimensions that are fundamental for so-called divided societies to build a common future together. The concept of "treaty federalism" has its roots in the pactist tradition, but also in that of political contracts as defined by thinkers of the pluralist school such as James Tully and Dimitrios Karmis. These authors, inspired by the customs of the English legal tradition, evoke the notion of "conventional constitutionalism" in order to explain the concept. These two concepts are usually used in an interchangeable manner. Long before the arrival of Europeans in America, First Nations did not hesitate to rely on the treaty formula to resolve disagreements with their rivals in neighbouring nations. Thus, the Iroquois, the Mi'kmaq, and the Blackfoot, just to name a few, had created associations that were federal in nature.[31]

The very idea of a treaty refers to the will of the parties coming to a negotiated agreement in the absence of coercion. It is also a form of advanced recognition of legitimate and equal-in-status partners that ensures the historical continuity of the nations that consented to the arrangements. James Tully speaks about conventional constitutionalism, treaty federalism, federal pluralism, or contractual federalism in a similar manner. Tully explains that pluralist federalism constitutes "a means of conciliation because it enables peoples mutually to recognise and reach agreement on how to assemble or federate the legal and political differences they wish to continue into the association."[32]

I am especially interested here in the concept of treaty federalism, which seems to evoke the will of political and social actors to respect the actual obligations of the partners.[33] Treaty federalism insists on the central place of political negotiations and on relations of cooperation between partners. This can be achieved on a bilateral basis, sometimes on a multilateral one, but never by adopting a unilateral approach. By offering a new basis of discussion, treaty federalism may lead actors towards dispute management. This management is not so much a question of accommodation, as it is of reconciliation, as is made clear in the work of Laforest and Gibbins regarding to Quebec–Canada relations following the 1995 referendum. Also, in the context of a proper and historically based treaty federalism, "the prevailing system of incorporation is transformed to a legitimate system of group recognition and rights in the Canadian constitution with the agreement of the indigenous peoples themselves."[34] It should be understood that this model applies to all the current cases involving situations of domination where one nation, or more, aspires to develop egalitarian relations.

Treaty federalism invites actors to undertake political negotiations rather than to take legal action in the courts, which is not only expensive, but often adopts the perspective of the encompassing state.[35] Tully invokes this idea when reminding us that "if the Crown pretends that the treaty negotiations take place within its overriding jurisdiction, then it fails to recognise the status of indigenous peoples, and incorporates and subordinates them without justification, rendering the negotiation illegitimate."[36] The idea expressed here is clear with regards to what treaty federalism opposes: any forced incorporation as well any form of subordination. To quote Tully again, "The presumption that jurisdiction must be exclusive is replaced with two (indigenous) principles: free and equal peoples on the same continent can mutually recognise the autonomy or sovereignty of each other in certain spheres and share jurisdictions."[37]

However, the nation states that evolved out of these original forms of government often sought to circumvent the agreements concluded with Aboriginal peoples that earlier governments had made.[38] Hence, for example, the Erasmus-Dussault commission, which reported on the precarious situation of Aboriginal peoples in Canada, specifies that "Aboriginal people are both Canadian citizens and citizens of their particular nations. Thus they hold a form of dual citizenship, which permits them to maintain loyalty to their nation and to Canada as a whole."[39] It is thus more urgent today than ever to propose corrective measures by reviving these agreements in the name of the principles of equality, equity, and the freedom of these nations.[40]

It is difficult to imagine means of inter-communal reconciliation that involve only instruments put in place by majority nations. Such instruments, created to manage diversity, were designed to ensure the economic and political interests of the majority nation and the encompassing state. These instruments act as an expression of a relation of power which has done a disservice to minority nations and which requires special attention on the part of social scientists. In an important study, jurist Sébastien Grammond notes how the central government in Canada has thwarted claims made by First Nations in much the same way as it did for the claims coming from the Quebec nation. Over the years, this tendency has led to the establishment of a new constitutional order in the country (1968–82). As Grammond observes:

> The basis of federal policy with regard to aboriginal people was similar to those which informed its Quebec policy: the search for individual equality and the rejection of special status founded on race, language or culture. The federal government deemed the laws, which had hitherto maintained a separation between aboriginal peoples and the rest of the population, embodied by the reservation system, had prevented the former from fully

taking part in Canadian society. It was thus necessary, in the long term, to abolish the legal status of Indian, and to put an end to their concentration on reservations by repealing the legislation.[41]

In this sense, a general policy of assimilation of Aboriginals, put in place by the central government, was pursued without overwhelming opposition until the beginning of the 1980s. Since then, in light of the tensions which occurred between the Aboriginal nations and the central government, and similar to those that opposed Quebec and Ottawa, Canadian politics has evolved somewhat.

The concepts of partnership and treaty federalism have made some inroads in terms of public debate as well as within political parties. Gradually, jurists and politicians have come to appreciate the importance of the concept of prior occupation of the land, which has given rise to claims made by First Nations. In the Van der Peet case, Supreme Court of Canada Justice Antonio Lamer wrote:

[T]he doctrine of aboriginal rights exists, and is recognized and affirmed by s.35 (1), because of one simple fact: when Europeans arrived in North America, aboriginal peoples *were already here*, living in communities on the land, and participating in distinctive cultures, as they had done for centuries. It is this fact, and this fact above all others, which separates aboriginal peoples from all other minority groups in Canadian society and which mandates their special legal, and now constitutional, status.[42]

Many are those for whom the central government's policy towards the Aboriginal peoples is too generous further believe that the concept of prior occupation should be disavowed. The work by Tom Flanagan entitled *First Nations? Second Thoughts*,[43] which constitutes the most virulent attack with regard to the claims of Aboriginal peoples, often supports what some would no doubt agree are arguments that border on racism, if not a kind of ethnocentrism.[44] These types of attacks have generally been badly received by political elites, particularly as Aboriginal peoples, given their precarious status throughout the world, have received for more than two decades support from many international organizations.

Pluralist or treaty federalism ought to gain the attention of all Québécois. However, it still seems difficult for many of them to move beyond the vision which was imposed by the central government since the Supreme Court of Canada was established as Canada's final court of appeal in 1949. It is possible to imagine various modes of management of diversity in a federal context. Moreover, it is true, as jurist Christophe Parent points out, that

> the state shows its limits and has proven incapable to allow greater freedom for nations. The legal theory of the state prohibits it from conceiving or making the smallest concession in terms of a right to secession within a federal multinational state. However, in a pact between nations, the right to secession is synonymous with the right to self-determination.[45]

Today, the lessons from *Beyond the Impasse*, require decision-makers to demonstrate political goodwill, and require social actors to show an exceptional capacity to mobilize. A return to the source of federalism (pactism, federal culture, treaty federalism), rather than the use of convenient formulas (typically imposed following wars, inter-communal conflicts, or strategic political alignments) seems to be the best way to deal with questions of community reconciliation, thus putting in place a new set of parameters to set debates on new constitutional grounds. This would also allow for the challenging of the current structure which supports the domination of the majority nation. In order to achieve this, a vast education campaign will be essential in order to sensitize non-Aboriginals regarding the merits of treaty federalism[46] and to convince Aboriginal peoples, although they have often paid the price for it in earlier decades, to once again trust these institutions. This way of thinking would lead to important advances in the area of intercultural exchange, a process which appears increasingly essential to engage in so as to open an authentic debate between partners, worthy of the name.

Conclusion: Embracing a New Politics of Dignity and Hospitality

> A denigration of a group identity, or its distortion, or its denial, ... the withholding of recognition or misrecognition is a form of oppression ... It is a form of inequality in its own right but also threatens the other form of equality, equal dignity, the fulfilment of which can be made impossible by stereotypes or a failure to recognize the self-definitional strivings of marginal groups.
>
> Tariq Modood[1]

Minority nations live in an age of great uncertainty. This age is characterized by the creation of a global market and economic standardization, by a rising tidal wave of cultural Americanization, by the decline of political literacy and civic engagement, by a growing uniformity between formerly distinct societies and cultures, and by the continuing atomization of the individual. Taken together, these phenomena constitute an unprecedented threat to the cultural and identitary survival of minority nations. Thus, there is a pressing need for these nations to reassert themselves and to resist the homogenizing imperatives of the age of uncertainty.

In this book, I have sought to identify how multinational polities can most effectively attend to the recognition of diversity and respond to the claims of minority nations. Since its inception, Canada has had to address these issues, and so the Canadian case provides an informative account of the manner in which minority and majority nations have been engaged in an evolving institutional and ideational dialogue. In turn, I have attempted to induce, from this particular context, broader lessons that may be applied both to other federal polities and to states undergoing the process of federalization. The Canadian and the Spanish cases provide the launching point from which I outline, in this concluding chapter, a new model for the persistence of minority nations.

In doing so, I will also attempt to outline the principles that are vital to ensure that national minorities and national majorities coexist under the auspices of just and equitable intercommunal relations and through which minority nations can fulfil their legitimate and democratic aspirations.

As seen in chapter 5, the relationship between international organizations and national minorities underwent a significant transformation between 1995 and 2005. Instead of promoting the rights of national minorities, as they once did, international organizations now focus on protecting the rights of individuals *within* minority nations.[2] To be sure, the plight of the national minorities of Kosovo and East Timor has been brought to public attention via the intermediary of international organizations.[3] However, these cases represent exceptions to the developing trend that has taken hold in the supranational sphere and this represented two exceptions, even though these international organizations agreed to stand up in favour of diversity in a world becoming more and more globalized. This development is perhaps best captured in a 2004 United Nations Development Programme report bearing the title *Cultural Liberty in Today's Diverse World*.[4]

In order to ensure their long-term survival, national minorities must overcome another hurdle. National majorities have historically downplayed or ignored national minority claims making on the pretext that it would threaten their shared state's position in international organizations and in international economic competition. Alain Renaut has effectively synthesized this argument: "Henceforth, differences between nation-states, that once were the locus of relationships of discrimination and exclusion between a dominant group and cultural minorities, are threatened by a trans-national process that seeks to level any impediment to the enshrinement of a global identity."[5] Faced with these threats, representatives of the encompassing state have demanded the unquestioned loyalty of national minorities. However, within the context of unfettered cultural and economic globalization, the dual threat of cultural erosion and declining international relevance is potentially far more devastating for minority nations. These nations must not only counteract the homogenizing forces of globalization, they must also resist the pressure of cultural uniformity generated from within their own state.

The loyalty and unity that national majorities demand of national minorities cannot be tolerated unless it is also reflected in the adoption of commensurate measures meant to ensure the enshrinement of liberty, freedom, and democracy within the multinational polity. Here the words of Lord Acton resonate across time. He argued that modern multinational federalism entails finding a balance between unity and liberty. Avoiding the reconciliation of these two ideas would have deleterious consequences on any state. On the one hand, despotism would prove to be the logical outcome if the goals of unity were served at the expense of liberty. On the other hand, the entrenchment of liberty without recognition for unity would inevitably lead to anarchy. For Lord Acton, the institutionalization of multinational federalism presented a means to avoid both of these paths: "The presence of different nations under the same sovereignty ... provides against the servility which flourishes under the shadow of a single authority, by balancing interests, multiplying associations, and giving to the subject the restraint and support of a combined opinion ... Liberty provokes diversity, and diversity preserves liberty by supplying the means of organisation."[6]

In this conclusion, I offer my own take on how liberty, diversity, and unity can be reconciled in the age of uncertainty. In turn, I hope to provide the contours of a new political project for multinational states that is rooted in the ideals of *liberty*, *recognition*, and *empowerment*. I contend that a political project based on these ideals will open new avenues for minority and majority nations to engage in frank and honest dialogue and will allow for the mutual and compatible enshrinement of difference, trust, and liberal communitarianism.[7] However, the adoption of this new political project is not a given. It will require that minority nations follow the path laid before them by indigenous movements and, in turn, resist with aplomb those who seek to perpetuate the status quo.

Towards a New Emancipatory Politics in Multinational Polities: Moderation, Dignity, and Hospitality

The enshrinement of a new political project for multinational polities requires cultivating three principles: the principle of moderation, the principle of dignity, and the principle of hospitality. These three principles are the fibres that, when sown together, create the canvas of a politics based on liberty, recognition, and empowerment.

The Principle of Moderation

Montesquieu's excursus on creating "balance" in political societies provides the theoretical basis for this first principle. In the eighteenth century, Montesquieu argued both for the separation of legislative, executive, and judicial powers and for the unrelenting pursuit of diversity. The principle of balance, which underlies both of these concepts, is vital for the enshrinement of a new politics within the context of the age of uncertainty. Balance, according to Montesquieu, is a necessary buttress against the development of autocratic, totalitarian, and tyrannical systems of government. As such, the entrenchment of balance and "good government" via the intermediary of the separation of powers and the pursuit of diversity necessitates that political ambitions and intentions be tempered or "moderated."

History is, however, rife with countless instances where political actors have defied the principle of moderation and, instead, have attempted to impose their will on constituents and political subjects. The First Nations of the New World have paid the price for the unfettered ambition of colonial powers. So too have minority nations been subject to the creation of structures of domination. This is most readily brought to light, within the Canadian context, by the landmark works of Eugenie Brouillet, John Conway, and Michel Seymour, which document the process of cultural, religious, and linguistic homogenization that the Quebec nation has had to endure since the foundation of the Canadian state.[8]

The Principle of Dignity

Great thinkers have also focused on human nature and the need for the creation of a just society. In particular, David Hume (1748) and John Rawls (1971) have addressed the need to design rules that lead to and sustain justice. In turn, Alain Renaut has attempted to apply these precepts to a modern context. In doing so, Renaut has translated Hume's "condition of justice" as the "condition of diversity." To cite Renaut: "I define the 'condition of diversity' as the totality of factors that have led contemporary societies to question the nature of the rules that they themselves must adopt in order to recognize that human nature is intrinsically differentiated and that it is only by acknowledging this fact that it can be treated with dignity."[9] This acknowledgment constitutes the basis for the second principle that must undergird international relations in modern democratic societies.

While the rhetoric of dignity is no longer a core component of majority–minority interaction in Canada, it is central to the persistent international conflict in another multinational polity. In recent years, Spain has borne witness to a growing conflict between nationalist forces and sub-state national movements in the Basque country, Catalonia, and Galicia.[10] The nature of this conflict is effectively captured in a comprehensive editorial (signed by twelve Catalan newspapers) published on 26 November 2009 (see Appendix).[11] The editorial strikes at the heart of the conflict between Bourbon nationalists based in Madrid and advocates of a plurinational Spain built on the model of multinational federalism.

> The foundational pacts that were then forged and that paved the way for the most virtuous thirty year period in Spanish history are now at stake. Having arrived at this point, it is essential to remember one of the principles at the core of our legal system, a principle stemming from Ancient Rome: *Pacta sunt servanda*, promises are binding ... Catalonia is worried, and it is important that all of Spain be aware of that fact. It is, in fact, more than worried ... Catalans these days are focusing, more than anything, on their dignity. This is worth keeping in mind.

These excerpts reveal that majority–minority relations are now at a turning point. Whether it is in Catalonia, in the Basque country, or in contexts where national minorities have engaged in similar political projects, the idea of dignity has become the rallying cry for the re-entrenchment of democracy. Rajeev Bhargava astutely articulates the importance of dignity:

> This worth [dignity] is "above all price," non-quantitative, "without equivalent," unsubstitutable, and irreplaceable and is grounded neither in heredity nor social rank ... Dignity is not earned. One has it simply because of one's potential to be a self-directing agent. If so, anything or anyone that denies or damages that potential, also undermines or deprives one of one's dignity. Moreover, since dignity is present in all, and cannot be there more or less, citizenship rights cannot be unequally distributed. If some people are excluded from standing for public office because of their religious affiliation, then this undermines their dignity.[12]

In recent years, many events have stirred passions in Spain. On 28 June 2010, Spain's Constitutional Tribunal gave a major blow to Catalonia's New Status as an autonomous region as the Tribunal modified a political deal agreed upon four years earlier by the Catalan and Spanish parliaments and by referendum in Catalonia. However, the important sections of the novel reform proposed by a new treaty between the central government and Catalonia were subsequently declared unconstitutional by the Constitutional Tribunal composed of jurists appointed by Spain's two major centrist political parties (the Socialist PSOE and the right-wing Partido popular). The Constitutional Tribunal declared several key components of the political deal unconstitutional, most notably that Catalonia itself cannot be considered a nation as stated in the preamble to the proposed New Status. Two weeks later, on the 10 July, Catalan civil society mobilized against the tribunal's ruling, adopted the rallying cry "We are a nation, we decide for ourselves," demanding that the Spanish government recognize Catalonia's parliamentary and popular sovereignty. A referendum is now being planned for 9 November 2014 against the will of the Spanish authorities. Although it is unclear at this point what the future holds for the Catalan people, we have nonetheless witnessed a return to national mobilization that rivals the power and numbers of those movements that emerged in the waning years of the Soviet empire. Within this more recent context, dignity is inextricably linked to the recognition of national diversity.

The Principle of Hospitality

The two first principles require that majority and minority nations alike embrace moderation and respect national dignity. The third principle that underlies the creation of a new political relationship between national groups requires that national minorities adopt an ethic of hospitality. The principle of hospitality is meant to enlarge contexts of choice and acts as a means to stop the atomizing effect of procedural liberalism.

Daniel Innerarity has recently devoted an entire volume to the idea of embracing an ethic of hospitality.[13] According to Innerarity, adopting hospitality as a prime imperative permits one "to appropriate an interpretive approach for understanding the rich strangeness of life, the ways of others, and the often opaque and hostile cultural context that we find ourselves immersed in and that, nonetheless, drives us to seek out what is new, to enter into contact with what is different and to seek out harmony in the disparity that constitutes our existence."[14] This way of understanding reality casts new light on the political world and gives primacy to a good life rooted in society and inter-communal relations.

The principle of hospitality will undoubtedly lead to significant intra-national uncertainty when deliberations will reach their crucial junctures. However, all mature democratic societies must embrace a certain degree of uncertainty and, accordingly, must be open to the possibility of change. It is only through inter-communal interaction that a modern society can implement a political project that listens to all voices and that encourages political participation within and across communities. Minority nations, more so than majority nations, must embrace the ethic of hospitality. They must address a series of challenges entailing, inter alia, the accommodation and integration of migrant populations, maintaining the predominance of majority languages, addressing the disappearance of a sense of community, counteracting citizen disengagement, and moderating the cultural and economic impact of globalization.[15] When confronted with these phenomena, minority nations are at risk of eroding. As such, they must find new ways of sustaining mobilization and activism both in the intra- and inter-national arenas.[16]

The principle of hospitality requires the adoption of a genuine politics of interculturalism.[17] The intercultural model allows for healthy dialogue between the constituent members of a diverse society and, in turn, for the articulation of an authentic pact between groups. On the one hand, this model also allows for the continued cultural and ideational diversification of the national minority. On the other hand, it provides an opportunity for the national minority to persist over time. While intercommunal dialogue may lead to the voicing of profound ideological disagreements, interculturalism is a necessary mechanism for ensuring the survival and democratic evolution of minority nations. As Daniel Innerarity states, "The renovation of democracy will not come from a passion for consensus but from the culture of reasonable disagreement. Democracy is impossible without some consensus, but it must also allow the expression of differences and the makeup of the collective identities of differentiated positions."[18]

Although this model has yet to catch on across modern democratic nation states, the two major national contexts, Catalonia and Quebec, have proved to be at the vanguard of a move towards the entrenchment of moderation, hospitality, and dignity as mechanisms for managing and reconciling diversity. In turn, the commitment to innovation, and the patience and determination demonstrated by these nations over the last three centuries evidences their unwavering adherence to Enlightenment principles and, concomitantly, suggests that they may offer a unique perspective on means and ways to deepen democracy at onset of the third millennium.

Appendix

The Dignity of Catalonia

On 26 November 2009, the following editorial was published simultaneously by twelve newspapers in Catalonia, including *Avui*, *La Vanguardia*, *El Punt*, and *El Periódico de Catalunya*.

After nearly three years of slow deliberations and constant tactical measures that have damaged its cohesion and eroded its prestige, the Constitutional Tribunal of Spain seems to be on the verge of ruling on the Catalan Statute of Autonomy, promulgated on July 20, 2006, by the Head of State, King Juan Carlos, with the following preface: "Let it be known: That the Cortes Generales [Spanish Parliament] have passed, the citizens of Catalonia have ratified in referendum, and I sanction the following constitutional law." This will be the first time since the restoration of democracy in 1977 that the Highest Court will rule on a constitutional law approved by a majority of voters. Expectations are high.

Expectations are high, and there is no little concern in the face of evidence that certain events have pushed the Constitutional Tribunal to act like a fourth Chamber, in confrontation with the Catalan Parliament, the Spanish Parliament, and the will of the people as expressed freely at the polls.

We must repeat that this is a new situation for the democracy. There are, however, additional reasons for concern. Of the twelve justices who are on the court, only ten can render judgment, since one (Pablo Pérez Tremps) was recused after a clumsy manoeuvre clearly meant to change the balance of the debate and another (Roberto García-Calvo) is no longer living. Of the ten justices able to vote, four remain in their position even though their term has expired. This is because of a shameful disagreement between the central government and the opposition over the timely replacement of judges for an institution recently described by Prime Minister José Luis Rodríguez Zapatero as "the heart of the democracy." It is a heart with blocked arteries, since only half its current members are free of judicial missteps or extended mandates. This is the Court of Cassation that will be rendering judgment on the Statute of Catalonia. Out of respect for the court – a respect that is without a doubt superior to the respect the court has shown itself on various occasions – we will not discuss the causes for the delay in the ruling any further.

The definition of Catalonia as a nation in the preamble to the new Statute, with the resulting evocation of "national symbols" (Section Two of the Spanish Constitution does recognize a Spain made up of regions and nationalities, does it not?), the right and duty to know the Catalan language, the organization of Judicial Power in Catalonia, and the relationship between the Spanish State and the Generalitat are among the most obvious points of tension in the debate, according to what has been heard, since a significant portion of the court seems to be opting for intransigent positions. There are those who once again dream of radical surgeries that would destroy the roots of Spanish complexity. This could, unfortunately, be the touchstone for the ruling.

Let us be clear: the true dilemma is between moving forward and moving backward; between accepting or blocking the democratic maturity of a plural Spain. What is at stake is not simply some particular article or another; what is at stake is the constitutional dynamic itself: the very spirit of 1977, which made a peaceful transition to democracy possible. There are serious motives for concern, since the ruling on the Statute could lead to a true institutional shutdown. This defensive tactic would be contrary to the maximum virtue of the Constitution: its open and integrative nature. The Constitutional Tribunal, therefore, will not merely be deciding the case brought by the Partido Popular (PP) against one of the State's constitutional laws. (This same PP is now attempting to achieve a rapprochement with Catalan society through constructive discourse and a flattering attitude.)

The Constitutional Tribunal will be ruling on the true extent of the Spanish frame of coexistence, in other words, on the most important legacy that the citizens who lived through and steered the regime change at the end of the 1970s will transmit to younger generations. These younger citizens who were educated in freedom and are fully

integrated into the complex supranationality of Europe are confronting the challenges of a globalization that relativizes the most rigid borders of the old Nation States. The foundational pacts that were then
forged and that paved the way for the most virtuous thirty-year period
in Spanish history are now at stake. Having arrived at this point, it
is essential to remember one of the principles at the core of our legal
system, a principle stemming from Ancient Rome: *Pacta sunt servanda*,
promises are binding.

Catalonia is worried, and it is important that all of Spain be aware
of that fact. It is, in fact, more than worried. It is increasingly fed up
with having to suffer the angry gaze of those who continue to view
Catalan identity (its institutions, economic structure, language, and
cultural traditions) as the design flaw that prevents Spain from achieving a dreamed of but impossible uniformity.

Catalans pay their taxes (without foral privilege);[1] they contribute
with their efforts to the transfer of revenues to the poorer regions of
Spain; they confront economic internationalization without the considerable benefits received by the Spanish capital, Madrid. Catalans
speak a language with a larger demographic base than that of several
of the official languages in the European Union, a language that, rather
than being loved, is so frequently subjected to obsessive scrutiny on the
part of official Spanish nationalism. Catalans respect the law, of course,
without renouncing their proven capacity for peaceful civic resistance.
Catalans these days are focusing, more than anything, on their dignity.
This is worth keeping in mind.

We are on the brink of a very important ruling. We hope that when
the Constitutional Tribunal makes their decision, they heed the specific
circumstances of the matter at hand – which is nothing but the demand
for improved self-government by an ancient European people. They
must remember that there is no absolute justice, only the justice of the
concrete case, which is why caution is the supreme legal virtue. Let us
remember: the Statute is the result of a double political pact supported
by the people through a referendum.

Let no one be fooled. Let no one misunderstand the inevitable contra-
dictions of present-day Catalonia. Let no one misinterpret the situation:
no matter the extent of problems, unhappiness, and difficulties, we are

---

1 Foral privileges, or *fueros*, correspond to rights going back to feudal times. They currently guarantee a special fiscal status to the Basque country as a historic nation.

not facing a weak, prostrate society that is willing to watch impassively as its dignity is undermined. We do not wish to presume a negative outcome, and we trust in the integrity of the judges, but no one who knows Catalonia will question that the recognition of identity, the improvement of self-government, the procurement of proper financing, and a qualitative leap in the management of infrastructures are being and will continue to be claimed tenaciously and with very broad political and social support. If necessary, Catalan solidarity will again articulate the legitimate response of a responsible society.

Editorial translated by Sandra Kingery,
Lycoming College

Notes

Introduction

1 Alain Dieckhoff, "L'état face au défi de la multinationalité," in Alain-G. Gagnon and Jocelyn Maclure, eds, *Repères en mutation: Identité et citoyenneté dans le Québec contemporain* (Montreal: Québec Amérique, Débats collection, 2001), 348.

2 Nicholas Tarling, *Historians and Southeast Asian History* (Auckland, NZ: Asia Institute, University of Auckland, 2000); Marc Ferro, ed., *Le livre noir du colonialism, XVe–XXIe siècle: De l'extermination à la repentance* (Paris: Robert Laffont, 2003).

3 M. Crawford Young, *Revisiting Nationalism and Ethnicity in Africa* (Los Angeles: Regents of the University of California, 2001).

4 Louis L. Snyder, *Macro-Nationalisms: A History of the Pan-Movements* (Westport, CT: Praeger, 1984).

5 Thanks to Paul May for his insight on this point.

6 Kenneth McRoberts, *Misconceiving Canada: The Struggle for National Unity* (Toronto: Oxford University Press, 1997); Michael Hechter, *Internal Colonialism: The Celtic Fringe in British National Development, 1535–1966* (London: Routledge, 1975); Montserrat Guibernau, *Catalan Nationalism: Francoism, Transition and Democracy* (London: Routledge, 2004); Michael Keating, *Nations against the State: The New Politics of Nationalism in Quebec, Catalonia and Scotland*, 2nd ed. (Basingstoke: Palgrave Macmillan, 2001).

7 The term "nation without a state" is a valid descriptor, but does not truly apply to the case of Quebec; this nation has its own political, cultural, economic, and social institutions.

8 Montserrat Guibernau, *Nations without States: Political Communities in a Global Age* (Cambridge: Polity Press, 1999).

9 I am indebted to Joseph Yvon Thériault for this conceptualization (see chapter 3).

10 See Alain-G. Gagnon, *The Case for Multinational Federalism: Beyond the All-Encompassing Nation* (London: Routledge, 2010).

11 Daniel Turp, "Statut d'autonomie de la Catalogne: Un ordre constitutionnel imposé, comme au Québec," *Le Devoir*, 16 July 2010, A9 (author's translation).

12 For additional informations for these two documentaries, refer to Dolors Genovès, *Adéu Espanya?* (Barcelona: Televisio de Catalunya, 2010) and Roger Boire and Jean-Pierre Roy, *Questions nationales* (Montreal: Production L'oeil fou, 2009).

13 See Michael Keating's and John McGarry's work on minority nations in the age of globalization: *Minority Nationalism and the Changing International Order* (Oxford: Oxford University Press, 2001). See also Alain-G. Gagnon, André Lecours, and Geneviève Nootens, eds, *Contemporary Majority Nationalism* (Montreal and Kingston: McGill-Queen's University Press, 2011).

14 Miquel Caminal i Badia, *El federalismo pluralista: Del federalismo nacional al federalismo plurinacional* (Barcelona: Paidos, 2002).

15 Pierre-Joseph Proudhon, "Du principe fédératif," *Oeuvres complètes*, volume *Du principe fédératif. La fédération et l'unité en Italie: Nouvelles observations sur l'unité italienne* (Paris: Marcel Rivière, 1959, part 1) (author's translation). See also Dimitrios Karmis, "Pourquoi lire Proudhon aujourd'hui? Le fédéralisme et le défi de la solidarité dans les sociétés divisées," *Politique et Sociétés* 21, no. 1 (2002), 43–65.

16 For an excellent study on this subject, see Bruce Gilley, *The Right to Rule: How States Win and Lose Legitimacy* (New York: Columbia University Press, 2009). See also Arend Lijphart, *Thinking about Democracy: Power Sharing and Majority Rule in Theory and Practice* (London: Routledge, 2008).

17 Enric Fossas, "Autonomy and Multinationality in Spain: Twenty-Five Years of Constitutional Experience," in Gagnon, Lecours, and Nootens, eds, *Comtemporary Majority Nationalism*, 197–209; Miquel Caminal and Josep Pich, "Federalisme i catalanisme (1868–2010)," *Activitat parlamentaria* 21 (April 2010), 8–15; Ferran Requejo, "L'estat de les autonomies, 25 anys desprès" *Nous Horitzons* 175 (2004), 16–20.

18 See http://www.tribunalconstitucional.es/fr/resolucionesrecientes/Documents/SENTENCIA_RI_8045-2006.pdf. Percentage obtained by the "yes" side was 73.9%.

19 This point is well made by Salvador Cardús i Ros, "Ilusion y compromiso," *La Vanguardia*, 7 July 2010, 22.

20 "Cuatro anos de encarnizada batalla politica," *El Pais*, 16 April 2010. http://elpais.com/elpais/2010/04/16/actualidad/1271405842_850215.html.

21 John Loughlin, "British and French Nationalisms Facing the Challenges of European Integration and Globalization," in Gagnon, Lecours, and Nootens, eds, *Contemporary Majority Nationalism*, 130.

22 James Tully, *Strange Multiplicity: Constitutionalism in an Age of Diversity* (Cambridge: Cambridge University Press, 1995), 8–9.

23 Anthony D. Smith, *Nations and Nationalism in a Global Era* (Cambridge: Polity Press, 1995), 86: "We may term a state a 'nation-state' only if and when a single ethnic and cultural population inhabits the boundaries of a state, and the boundaries of that state are coextensive with the boundaries of that ethnic and cultural population."

24 Daniel J. Elazar, *Exploring Federalism* (Tusculoosa: University of Alabama Press, 1987).

25 Quebec's struggle for national self-determination is often invoked by national minorities in Asia, Latin America, and Spain, in so far as it offers a beacon of hope for other groups living within a liberal, democratic, plurinational context. See François Taglioni, "Les revendications séparatistes et autonomistes au sein des territoires mono- et multi-insulaires: Essai de typologie," *Cahiers de géographie du Québec* 49 (April 2005), 6–18; and Stéphane Guillaume, *La question du Tibet en droit international* (Paris: L'Harmattan, 2009). And see, among others, Alejandro Saiz Arnaiz, *Estado federal i estatuto particular: La posicion constitucional de la provincia de Quebec en la federacion canadiense* (Madrid: Instituto Vasco de Administracion Publica, 1997); and Montserrat Guibernau, *Per un catalanisme cosmopolita* (Barcelona: Editorial Angle, 2009).

26 Reference regarding the secession of Québec, [1998] 2 R.C.S. 217. http://www.canlii.org/en/ca/scc/doc/1998/1998canlii793/1998canlii793.pdf. The underlining is present in the original text.

27 Hector Bofill, *La Democràcia Cuirassada* (Barcelona: Esfera des llibres, 2005).

28 Daniel Turp, *La nation bâillonnée* (Montreal: VLB éditeur, 2000).

29 Michael Keating, *Nations against the State*; Scott L. Greer, *Nationalism and Self-Government: The Politics of Autonomy in Scotland and Catalonia* (Albany: State University of New York Press, 2008); Montserrat Guibernau, *The Identity of Nations* (Cambridge: Polity, 2007).

30 Éric Montpetit, *Le fédéralisme d'ouverture: La recherche d'une légitimité canadienne au Québec* (Quebec: Septentrion, 2007). See also Alain-G. Gagnon and Raffaele Iacovino, *Federalism, Citizenship, and Quebec: Debating Multinationalism* (Toronto: University of Toronto Press, 2007).

31 Craig Calhoun, *Nations Matter: Culture, History, and the Cosmopolitan Dream* (London: Routledge, 2007), 152–7.

32 Marc Chevrier, "La démocratie, ses empires et le Dominion multiculturel canadien," *Médiane* 3, no. 2 (2008), 42. Author's translation.

33 This will be addressed in greater detail in chapter 2.

34 Will Kymlicka, "Multinational Federalism in Canada: Rethinking the Partnership," in Guy Laforest and Roger Gibbins, eds, *Beyond the Impasse: Toward Reconciliation* (Montreal: Institute for Research on Public Policy, 1998), 15–50.

35 Paolo Dardanelli, "Multinational Switzerland?" *Swiss Political Science Review* 14, no. 3 (2008), 551–77.

36 Graham Fraser, *Annual Report 2009–2010, Beyond Obligations* (Ottawa: Office of the Commissioner of Official Languages, Minister of Public Works and Government Services Canada, 2010), vol. 1: 24–6.

37 Guy Lachapelle, ed., *Diversité culturelle, identités et mondialisation. De la ratification à la mise en oeuvre de la convention sur la diversité culturelle* (Quebec: Les Presses de l'Université Laval, 2008).

38 See Will Kymlicka, "The Internationalization of Minority Rights," in Sujit Choudhry, ed., *Constitutional Design for Divided Societies* (Oxford: Oxford University Press, 2008), 114–26.

1. Linguistic Diversity, Language Policy, and the Limits of Federal Accommodation

1 The first version of this chapter was presented in Ottawa on 13 May 2008 at a round table organized by the World Center on Pluralism (Aga Khan Foundation) on the Canadian experiment in the management of diversity.

2 Selma K. Sonntag, "La diversité linguistique et la mondialisation," *Politique et Sociétés* 29 (2010), 20.

3 See Joël Belliveau and Frédéric Boily, "Deux révolutions tranquilles? Transformations politiques et sociales au Québec et au Nouveau-Brunswick (1960–1967)," *Recherches sociographiques* 46, no. 1 (2005), 11–34. See also the influential works of Linda Cardinal, in particular *Le fédéralisme asymétrique et les minorités linguistiques et nationales* (Sudbury, ON: Éditions Prise de parole, 2008).

4 Garth Stevenson, *Parallel Paths: The Development of Nationalism in Ireland and Quebec* (Montreal: McGill-Queen's University Press, 2006).

5 See André Raynauld, Gérald Marion, and Richard Béland, "The Distribution of Income in Canada among Ethnic Groups," *Research Report prepared for the Royal Commission on Bilingualism and Biculturalism*, 1966.

6 Kenneth D. McRae, "The Principle of Territoriality and the Principle of Personality in Multilingual States," *International Journal of the Sociology of Language* 4 (1975), 35–54 ; Jean Laponce, *Language and Their Territories* (Toronto: University of Toronto Press, 1987).

7 *Preliminary Report of the Royal Commission on Bilingualism and Biculturalism* (Ottawa: Queen's Printer, 1965), 135.

8 The Quebec government tabled, in the Fall of 2012, a new language bill (Bill 14) that would also include businesses of 25 to 49 employees. Following the election of the Liberal party on 7 April 2014, it is still unclear what new actions, if any, will be taken by the Couillard government in this sector.

9 Robert Dutrisac, "Québec bafoue la Charte de la langue," *Le Devoir*, 17 April 2008, A1–8; Michel David, "Une sinistre farce," *Le Devoir*, 17 April 2008, A3.

10 See Angéline Martel, "La politique linguistique canadienne et québécoise. Entre stratégies de pouvoir et d'identités," *Globe, Revue internationale d'études québécoises* 2, no. 2 (1999), 1–26.

11 Government of Canada, *Report of the Royal Commission on Bilingualism and Biculturalism, Book III, The Work World* (Ottawa: Queen's Printer, 1969).

12 For example, Québécois accounted for 29 per cent of the Canadian constituency in 1945 and, at that time, held only 12.5 per cent of public services jobs. In 1971, we see a marginal improvement, with 15 per cent of intermediate public service positions held by francophones. For a more detailed study, see Alain-G. Gagnon, Luc Turgeon, with Olivier De Champlain, "La bureaucratie représentative au sein des états multinationaux," *Revue française d'administration publique* 2, no. 118 (2006), 291–306. See also Léon Dion, "Towards a Self-Determined Consciousness," in Dale C. Thomson, ed., *Quebec: Society and Politics: A View From the Inside* (Toronto: McClelland & Stewart, 1973), 26–38.

13 Jorge Niosi, *La bourgeoisie canadienne: La formation et le développement d'une classe dominante* (Montreal: Boréal Express, 1979).

14 Maurice Saint-Germain, *Une économie à libérer: Le Québec analysé dans ses structures économiques* (Montreal: Les Presses de l'Université de Montréal, 1973).

15 Marc Levine, *The Reconquest of Montreal: Language Policy and Social Change in a Bilingual City* (Philadelphia: Temple University Press, 1991).

16 Daniel Latouche, "Le pluralisme ethnique et l'agenda public au Québec," *Revue internationale d'action communautaire* 21 (1989), 11–23.

17 Official Languages Act, 1968–1969, S.R.C. 1970, ch. 0–2, art. 2

18 Required qualifications are often times minimal. Office of the Commissioner of Official Languages, Annual Report Special Edition 35th

Anniversary 1969–2004, vol. 1. http://epe.lac-bac.gc.ca/100/201/301/ra_commissaire_langues/html/ra04/v1/2004_05_e.htm.

19 Ibid.

20 Kenneth D. McRae, "Bilingual Language Districts in Finland and Canada: Adventures in the Transplanting of an Institution," *Canadian Public Policy* 4, no. 3 (1978), 331–51. A new constraint has emerged with the federal government's decision to abandon the mandatory long-form census. This decision led the director of Statistics Canada, Munir Sheikh, to hand in his resignation on 21 July 2010.

21 See Éric Guntermann, "La résistance au nationalisme linguistique: Une comparaison entre le Québec et la Catalogne," unpublished master's thesis, Institut d'Études Politiques de Paris, 2009. The author highlights the counter-mobilizational strategies of anglophones in Quebec and Castilla-nophones in Catalonia.

22 Luc Turgeon, "La grande absente: La société civile au coeur des changements de la Révolution tranquille," *Globe, Revue internationale d'études québécoises* 2, no. 1 (1999), 35–56.

23 See Gérard Bergeron, *Notre miroir à deux faces Trudeau, Lévesque ... et forcément avec bien d'autres* (Montreal: Québec Amérique, 1985).

24 Simone Azzam and Marie Mc Andrew, *Évaluation des services offerts dans le cadre du PELO et de l'impact de ce programme sur les élèves et les écoles à la CECM* (Montreal: Commission des écoles catholiques de Montréal, 1987), 105–6.

25 These debates have not stopped since the adoption of Bill 101. One of the most recent debates involves "les écoles passerelles," which led to the adoption of Bill 103 in the Spring of 2010.

26 John A. Dickinson and Brian Young, *A Short History of Quebec* (Toronto: Copp Clark Pitman, 1993).

27 Gagnon, *The Case for Multinational Federalism*.

28 See Marie-Ève Hudon, *Language Regimes in the Provinces and Territories* (Ottawa: Legal and Legislative Affairs Division, Parliamentary Information and Research Service, Library of Parliament, 20 July 2011). http://www.parl.gc.ca/Content/LOP/ResearchPublications/2011-66-e.pdf.

29 No data is avaible on language transfers from French to English. Data on languages spoken at home were first collected in 1971.

30 Louise Marmen and Jean-Pierre Corbeil, *Nouvelles perspectives canadiennes. Les langues au Canada, Recensement de 2001*, Ministère des Travaux publics et Services gouvernementaux, 2004; Statistics Canada, Census 2006: 97-555-XIF.

31 Statistics Canada, *Le portrait linguistique en évolution*, Census 2006: 97-555-XIF.

32 Conrad Sabourin and Julie Bernier, *Government Responses to Language Issues: Canadian Examples* (Office of the Language Commissioner of Nunavut, 2001), p. 62.

33 For a comparison between linguistic minorities in Quebec and New Brunswick, see James T. Coughlin, "Lobbying for Language: Alliance Québec, the Société des Acadiens du Nouveau-Brunswick and Federal Conciliation in Minority Language Rights," honours essay (Ottawa: Department of Political Science, Carleton University, 1986).

34 Mother tongue: Inuktitut 20185 (69.54%); English 7765 (26.75%); French 370 (1.27%); Inuinnaqtun 295 (1.02%). Source: Census 2006.

35 See *Inuit Language Protection Act*, SNu 2008, c. 17, http://www.canlii.org/en/nu/laws/stat/snu-2008-c-17/latest/snu-2008-c-17.html.

36 See *Consolidation of Inuit Language Protection Act* (2008), http://langcom.nu.ca/sites/langcom.nu.ca/files/consSNu2008c17.pdf.

37 For a more detailed study, see Jean-Claude Corbeil, *De l'embarras des langues: Origine, conception, évolution de la politique linguistique québécoise* (Montreal: Québec Amérique, 2008).

38 Government of Nunavut, *Inuit Language Protection Act: Backgrounder*, http://www.gov.nu.ca/news/2008/september/sept19a.pdf.

39 Louis-Jacques Dorais, "Discours et identité à Iqaluit après l'avènement du Nunavut," *Études Inuit* 30, no. 2 (2006), 172–5.

40 See *Catalan, Language of Europe* (Barcelona: Generalitat de Catalunya, Departament de la Vicepresidència, Secretaria de Política Lingüística). http://www20.gencat.cat/docs/Llengcat/Documents/Publicacions/Catala%20llengua%20Europa/Arxius/cat_europa_angles_07.pdf.

41 *Entente de coopération en matière linguistique entre le gouvernement du Québec et le gouvernement autonome de la Catalogne* (Quebec: Ministère des Relations internationales, 1996).

42 Will Kymlicka, *Multicultural Citizenship: A Liberal Theory of Minority Rights* (Oxford: Oxford University Press, 1995).

43 Kenneth McRoberts, "Cultures, Language, and Nations: Conceptions and Misconceptions," unpublished paper presented to the 16th Annual London Conference for Canadian Studies, Birkbeck College, University of London, 26 February 2000, p. 25. http://www.mrifce.gouv.qc.ca/calendrier/document/614_McRoberts.pdf.

44 Kymlicka, "Multinational Federalism," in Laforest and Gibbins, eds, *Beyond the Impasse*, 23.

2. New Challenges for Multinational States

1 The very first elements of this chapter were put together at a conference held in Brussels during the XXI Biennial of the French Language in May 2005. New elements were added when I gave a series of conferences in Beijing and Shanghai in March 2011.

2 *Building the Future: A Time for Reconciliation* (Quebec: Gouvernement du Québec, 2008), 134.

3 For a more in-depth analysis of current trends see Miquel Caminal and Ferran Requejo, eds, *Federalisme i plurinacionalitat: Teoria i anàlisi de casos* (Barcelona: Institut d'Estudis Autonomics, Clàssics del Federalisme collection, 2009), in particular chapters written by Ferran Requejo, Philip Resnick, Wilfried Swenden, Stephen Tierney, and Miquel Caminal.

4 See Michel Seymour, ed., *La reconnaissance dans tous ses états: repenser les politiques de pluralisme culturel* (Montreal: Québec Amérique, Débats collection, 2009). In particular, see Michel Seymour and Jean-Philippe Royer, "Les nations comme sujets de reconnaissance," 157–98. Also, Michel Seymour, ed., *The Plural States of Recognition* (Basingstoke: Palgrave Macmillan, 2010).

5 See Daniel Salée, "Enjeux et défis de l'affirmation identitaire et politique des peuples autochtones au Canada," *Journal of Canadian Studies* 26 (Fall 2002), 143.

6 Claude Hagège, *Halte à la mort des langues* (Paris: Odile Jacob, 2000). Author's translation.

7 For an astute exploration of the decline of nation states, see Susan Strange, *The Retreat of the State: The Diffusion of Power in the World Economy* (Cambridge: Cambridge University Press, 2000 [1996]).

8 For further conceptual analysis of this phenomenon, see Hélène Ruiz Fabri, "Maîtrise du territoire et rôle international de l'État," *Revue de l'Académie des sciences morales et politiques* 1 (2000), 88.

9 Raoul Marc Jennar, "Ces accords que Bruxelles impose à l'Afrique. Une Europe toujours à construire," *Le monde diplomatique*, February 2005, 10.

10 Jennar, *Europe, La trahison des élites* (Paris: Fayard, 2004), 10. Author's translation.

11 See Jennar's analysis, ibid., 10.

12 See Alain Noël and Alain-G. Gagnon, "Le monde, les régions, la nation: vers une nouvelle définition de l'espace québécois," *L'Espace québécois* (Montreal: Québec Amérique, 1995), pp. 18–19.

13 Jacques Beauchemin, Gilles Bourque, and Jules Duchastel have clearly identified this problem in their analysis of neo-liberal discourse and its

relation to social regulatory policy; see "Du providentialisme au néo-libéralisme: De Marsh à Axworthy. Un nouveau discours de légitimation de la régulation sociale," *Cahiers de recherche sociologique* 24 (1995), 45–6.

14 The works of Peter Katzenstein on the effective development of industrial policy in small European states has proved to be invaluable in the articulation of these answers. See Peter Katzenstein, *Small States in World Markets: Industrial Policy in Europe* (Ithaca: Cornell University Press, 1985). Also Alberto Alesina and Edward Spolaore, *The Size of Nations* (Cambridge, MA: MIT Press, 2003).

15 Gilley, *The Right to Rule*, see chapter 2, "Sources of Legitimacy," 29–57.

16 For an excellent literature review, see Benoît Lévesque, "Repenser l'économie pour contrer l'exclusion sociale: De l'utopie à la nécessité," in Juan-Luis Klein et Benoît Lévesque, eds, *Contre l'exclusion: Repenser l'économie* (Quebec: Les Presses de l'Université du Québec, 1995), 17–44.

17 See Jane Jenson and Susan Phillips, "Regime Shift: New Citizenship Practices in Canada," *International Journal of Canadian Studies* 14 (Fall 1996), 111–36.

18 Jane Jenson, "Recognising Difference: Distinct Societies, Citizen Regimes and Partnership," in Laforest and Gibbins, eds, *Beyond the Impasse*, 218.

19 Philip Resnick, "Toward a Multinational Federalism: Asymmetrical and Confederal Alternatives," in F. Leslie Seidle, ed., *Seeking a New Canadian Partnership: Asymetrical and Confederal Options* (Montreal: Institute for Research on Public Policy, 1994), 71–89. See also Alain-G. Gagnon and James Tully, eds, *Multinational Democracies* (Cambridge: Cambridge University Press, 2001).

20 See Alain-G. Gagnon and Raffaele Iacovino, "Expanding the Boundaries of Citizenship," in Alain-G. Gagnon, ed., *Quebec State and Society* (Toronto: University of Toronto Press, 2004), 369–88.

21 For a Quebec/Wallonia comparasion, see Christophe Traisnel, "Le nationalisme de contestation: Le rôle des mouvements nationalistes dans la construction politique des identités wallonne et québécoise en Belgique et au Canada," unpublished doctoral thesis, Paris II–Université de Montréal, 2005. For Scotland, see Nicola McEwen, *Nationalism and the State: Welfare and Identity in Scotland and Quebec* (Brussels: Les Presses interuniversitaires européennes/Peter Lang, 2006).

22 Jenson, "Recognising Difference," 219–27.

23 Gilley, *The Right to Rule*, 29–57.

24 John F. Conway, *Debts to Pay: The Future of Canadian Federalism in Quebec*, 3rd ed. (Toronto: James Lorimer, 2004).

25 See Alain-G. Gagnon and Guy Lachapelle, "Québec Confronts Canada: Two Competing Societal Projects Searching for Legitimacy," *Publius* 26, no. 3 (1996), 177–91.

26 Michel Seymour, "On Not Finding Our Way: The Illusory Reform of the Canadian Federation," in A.-G. Gagnon, ed., *Contemporary Canadian Federalism* (Toronto: University of Toronto Press, 2009), 187–212.

27 See François Rocher, "The Quebec-Canada Dynamic or the Negation of the Ideal of Federalism," in Gagnon, ed., *Contemporary Canadian Federalism*, 81–131.

28 See Alain-G. Gagnon and Jacques Hérivault, "The Bloc Québécois: The Dynamics of a Distinct Electorate," in Jon H. Pammett and Christopher Dorman, eds, *The Canadian General Election of 2004* (Toronto: Dundurn Press, 2004), 139–69.

29 See James Tully on the imposition of a new constitutional order in Quebec without the province's consent: "Liberté et dévoilement dans les sociétés multinationales," *Globe, Revue internationale d'études québécoises* 2, no. 2 (1998), 31–2. For a comparative perspective on Quebec, Scotland, and Catalonia, see Stephen Tierney, *Constitutional Law and National Pluralism* (Oxford: Oxford University Press, 2005).

30 See Gagnon and Tully, eds, *Multinational Democracies*; see also Alain-G. Gagnon, Montserrat Guibernau, and François Rocher, eds, *The Conditions of Diversity in Multinational Democracies* (Montreal: McGill-Queen's University Press, 2003).

31 See the works of Daniel Innerarity on these themes. In particular, *The Future and Its Enemies: In Defense of Political Hope* (Stanford, CA: Stanford University Press, 2012).

32 David R. Cameron and Janice Gross Stein, "The State as Place amid Shifting Spaces," in D.R. Cameron and J. Gross Stein, eds, *Street Protest and Fantasy Parks* (Vancouver: UBC Press, 2002), 141–59.

33 Ibid., 149.

34 See Carles Casajuana, *Le dernier homme qui parlait catalan* (Paris: Robert Laffont, 2009), for a fictional account of the disappearance of a national language that may turn out to be all too real.

35 See Montserrat Guibernau, "Nations without States: Political Communities in the Global Age," *Michigan Journal of International Law* 25, no. 4 (2004), 1272–4. Here the author explores the potential consequences of a refusal to recognize and protect linguistic diversity.

3. The Pillars of Quebec's New Citizenship Regime

1 This chapter builds upon and refines an argument made originally at a conference organized by the Centre de recherche interdisciplinaire sur la diversité et la démocratie (CRIDAQ) following the publication of the

Bouchard-Taylor report, entitled *Building the Future: A Time for Reconciliation*. See http://www.accommodements-quebec.ca/documentation/rapports/rapport-final-integral-en.pdf.

2 Jane Jenson, "Recognising Difference: Distinct Societies, Citizenship Regimes and Partnership," in Guy Laforest and Roger Gibbins, eds, *Beyond the Impasse, Toward Reconciliation* (Montreal: Institute for Research on Public Policy, 1998), 215.

3 Bhikhu C. Parekh, *The Future of Multi-Ethnic Britain: Report of the Commission of the Future of Multi-Ethnic Britain* (London: Profile Books, 2000).

4 Gérard Bouchard and Charles Taylor, *Building the Future: A Time for Reconciliation* (Quebec: Gouvernement du Québec, 2008).

5 Council of Europe, *White Paper on Intercultural Dialogue: Living Together as Equals in Dignity* (Strasburg: Council of Europe, 2008). http://www.coe.int/t/dg4/intercultural/source/white%20paper_final_revised_en.pdf.

6 See Tsujimura (with co-editor Mari Osawa), *Gender Equality in Multicultural Societies: Gender, Diversity, and Conviviality in the Age of Globalization* (Sendai: Tohoku University Press, 2010).

7 Joseph Yvon Thériault, *Faire société: Société civile et espaces francophones* (Sudbury, ON: Prise de parole, 2007). Author's translation.

8 For example, the federal government's interventions into agriculture, health, and social services. See Éric Montpetit, "Can Quebec Neo-Corporatist Network Withstand Canadian Federalism and Internationalization?" in Alain-G. Gagnon, ed., *Quebec: State and Society*, 3rd ed. (Toronto: University of Toronto Press, 2004), 165–81.

9 See Raffaele Iacovino, "En matière de reconnaissance du pluralisme ethnoculturel, le Québec a-t-il les moyens de ses ambitions?" and Michel Seymour, "Une constitution interne comme remède au malaise identitaire québécois," in Gagnon, ed., *La diversité québécoise en débat*, 204–22 and 223–44.

10 Daniel Turp has proposed a law that would see the province adopt a constitution (tabled on 17 April 2007). Daniel Turp, *Constitution québécoise*, Bill 196 (draft), 1st session, 38th legislature (Quebec: Éditeur officiel du Québec, 2007).

11 This has reaffirmed the Gérin-Lajoie doctrine which has sought to increase Quebec's global presence in political and economic issues. See Stéphane Paquin, ed., *Les relations internationales du Québec depuis la Doctrine Gérin-Lajoie (1965–2005)* (Quebec: Les Presses de l'Université Laval, 2006).

12 According to available statistics, 63% of Québécois approve of Quebec's constitutional project (albeit within Canada); the level of support among francophones hovers at 69%, whereas it only reaches 37% among

non-francophones. The new constitution would emphasize the primacy of French, cultural heritage, gender equality, and secularism. See Sondage Léger Marketing, "L'opinion des Québécois à l'égard d'une Constitution du Québec," www.cyberpresse.ca, available at http://www.vigile. net/L-opinion-des-Quebecois-a-l-egard.

13 Bouchard and Taylor, *Building the Future*, 121.

14 The Quebec Secession Reference (1998) – the Supreme Court's decision concerning Quebec's right to secede – leads us to believe that the Supreme Court would have in fact rejected the repatriation of the Constitution in 1981–2 had Parliament not respected four fundamental principles outlined in the reference (see chapter 1).

15 Tully, "Liberté et dévoilement," 31.

16 See Eugénie Brouillet, *La négation de la nation: L'identité culturelle québécoise et le fédéralisme canadien* (Quebec: Septentrion, 2005). See also Marc Chevrier, "Federalism in Canada: A World of Competing Definitions and Views," in Stephen Tierney, ed., *Multiculturalism and the Canadian Constitution* (Vancouver: UBC Press, 2007), 108–26.

17 Stephen Tierney, "Crystallizing Dominance: Majority Nationalism, Constitutionalism and the Courts," in A. Lecours and G. Nootens, eds, *Dominant Nationalism, Dominant Ethnicity: Identity, Federalism and Democracy* (Brussels: Les Presses interuniversitaires européennes/Peter Lang, 2009), 95. See also Jan Erk and Alain-G. Gagnon, "Constitutional Ambiguity and Federal Trust: The Codification of Federalism in Belgium, Canada and Spain," *Regional and Federal Studies* 10, no. 1 (2000), 92–111.

18 Despite the failure of the Meech Lake Accord, we can nonetheless see that it helped to advance the cause of national autonomy in the realms of immigration and the recognition of Quebec as a distinct society.

19 See Alain-G. Gagnon and Joseph Garcea, "Quebec and the Pursuit of Special Status," in R.D. Olling and M.W. Westmacott, eds, *Perspectives on Canadian Federalism* (Scarborough: Prentice-Hall, 1988), 314–25.

20 See François Rocher and Micheline Labelle, "Immigration, Integration and Citizenship Policies in Canada and Quebec: Tug of War between Competing Societal Projects," in Ricard Zapata-Barrero, ed., *Immigration and Self-Government of Minority Nations* (Brussels: Peter Lang, Diversitas collection, 2009), 57–83.

21 See Michael Foley, *The Silence of Constitutions* (London, New York: Routledge, 1989). See also David Thomas's excellent *Whistling Past the Graveyard: Constitutional Abeyance, Quebec and the Future of Canada* (Toronto: Oxford University Press, 1997).

22 For a more recent take, see Stéphan Gervais, Dimitrios Karmis, and Diane Lamoureux, eds, *Du tricoté serré au métissé serré? La culture publique commune au Québec en débats* (Quebec: Les Presses de l'Université Laval, 2008).

23 Geneviève Nootens, "Penser la diversité: Entre monisme et pluralisme," in B. Gagnon, ed., *La diversité québécoise en débat*, 56–73.

24 See Àngel Castineira's study "Imagined Nations: Personal Identity, National Identity, and the Place of Memory," and John Coakley, "National Majorities in New States: Managing the Challenge of Diversity," in Gagnon, Lecours, and Nootens, eds, *Contemporary Majority Nationalism*, 43–79 and 101–24.

25 Donald Forbes, "Immigration and Multiculturalism vs. Quebec Separatism: An Interpretation of Canadian Constitutional Politics since 1968," paper presented at the American Political Science Association annual meeting (Chicago, 30 August 2007).

26 See Bernard Gagnon, ed., *La diversité québécoise en débat: Bouchard, Taylor et les autres* (Montreal: Québec Amérique, Débats collection, 2010).

27 See Arend Lijphart, *Democracy in Plural Societies: A Comparative Exploration* (New Haven: Yale University Press, 1977) and *Democracies: Patterns of Majoritarian and Consensus Government in Twenty-One Countries* (New Haven: Yale University Press, 1984).

28 For more on these subjects, see Gagnon, *The Case for Multinational Federalism*; and Ferran Requejo, ed., *Democracy and National Pluralism* (London: Routledge, 2001).

29 Yasmeen Abu-Laban and Daiva Stasiulis, "Ethnic Pluralism Under Siege: Popular and Partisan Opposition to Multiculturalism," *Canadian Public Policy* 18, no. 4 (1992), 365–86; V. Seymour Wilson, "The Tapestry Vision of Canadian Multiculturalism," *Canadian Journal of Political Science* 26, no. 4 (1993), 645–69.

30 Neil Bissoondath, *Selling Illusions: The Cult of Multiculturalism in Canada* (Toronto: Penguin Books, 1994).

31 Daniel Innerarity, *The Transformation of Politics: Governing in the Age of Complex Societies* (Brussels: Peter Lang, 2010), 79.

32 See introduction by Guy Laforest in Charles Taylor, *Reconciling the Solitudes: Essays on Canadian Federalism and Nationalism* (Montreal: McGill-Queen's University Press, 1993), x.

33 Reference could also be made here to recent work produced as part of the 4th Convention of the Quebec Association of Constitutional Law entitled "Perspectives québécoises sur le principe fédératif," Université de Montréal, 11 September 2009.

34 Stephen Tierney's work on this theme is particularly insightful. See Stephen Tierney, "Crystallizing Dominance: Majority Nationalism, Constitutionalism and the Courts," in Lecours and Nootens, eds, *Dominant Nationalism, Dominant Ethnicity*, 87–109.
35 See Peter H. Russell, "Trust and Distrust in Canada's Multinational Constitutional Politics," which was part of a seminar on trust and mistrust in plurinational societies, Research Group on Plurinational Societies, Université du Québec à Montréal, 4 June 2010.

4. From Containment to Empowerment

1 A very first version of this chapter was presented at Carlos III University of Madrid during my stay as visiting fellow in the Spring of 2010.
2 Isaiah Berlin, "Two Concepts of Liberty," in Henry Hardy, ed., *Liberty* (Oxford: Oxford University Press, 2002).
3 For more on the context of choices see Kymlicka, *Multicultural Citizenship*, 82–4.
4 See Philip Pettit, *Republicanism: A Theory of Freedom and Government* (Oxford: Clarendon Press, 1997), 97–106.
5 Ibid., 99.
6 See Charles Taylor, *Philosophy and the Human Sciences: Philosophical Papers 2* (Cambridge: Cambridge University Press, 1985). Many thanks to Dan Pfeffer, who has brought this text by Taylor to my attention.
7 For example, see Ferran Requejo, *Multinational Federalism and Value Pluralism: The Spanish Case* (London: Routledge, 2005) and Guy Laforest, *Pour la liberté d'une société distincte: Parcours d'un intellectuel engagé* (Quebec: Les Presses de l'Université Laval, 2004).
8 Alain-G. Gagnon and Richard Simeon, "Unity and Diversity in Canada: A Preliminary Assessment," in Luis Moreno and César Colino Cámara, eds, *Unity and Diversity in Federal Systems* (Montreal: McGill-Queen's University Press, 2010), 109–38.
9 Andrée Lajoie, "Federalism in Canada: Provinces and Minorities – Same Fight," in Gagnon, ed., *Contemporary Canadian Federalism* (Toronto: University of Toronto Press, 2009), 183–209.
10 Jean Leclair, "The Supreme Court of Canada's Understanding of Federalism: Efficiency at the Expense of Diversity," *Queen's Law Journal* 28 (2003), 411–53.
11 Lajoie, "Federalism in Canada."
12 François Chevrette and Herbert Marx, *Droit constitutionnel* (Montreal: Les Presses de l'Université de Montréal, 1982), 389.

13 The first two powers have fallen into disuse. However, they have contributed to the creation of a feeling about central government's natural domination of the political order. The power of disavowal was used 112 times and was abandoned in 1943. The power of reservation was used 70 times and abandoned in 1961.

14 See Andrée Lajoie's pioneering work, *Le pouvoir déclaratoire du Parlement, augmentation discrétionnaire de la compétence fédérale au Canada* (Montreal: Les Presses de l'Université de Montréal, 1969).

15 Edmond Orban, *La dynamique de centralisation dans l'État federal: Un processus irréversible?* (Montreal: Québec Amérique, 1984).

16 See, inter alia, Alain Noël, "General Study of the Framework Agreement," in Alain-G. Gagnon and Hugh Segal, eds, *The Canadian Social Union: 8 Critical Analyses* (Montreal: McGill-Queen's University Press, 2000), 9–35. In the same volume, see also Claude Ryan, "The Agreement on the Canadian Social Union as Seen by a Quebec Federalist," 209–26; and André Tremblay, "Federal Spending Power," 155–88.

17 This strategy has a lot in common with Léon Dion's (Stéphane Dion's father) strategy during the Bélanger-Campeau commission inquiry on the future of Quebec within the Canadian federation which he described as a "knife to the throat" approach. See Alain-G. Gagnon and Daniel Latouche, *Allaire, Bélanger, Campeau et les autres: Les Québécois face à leur avenir* (Montreal: Québec Amérique, 1991).

18 Stéphane Dion, "Belgique et Canada: Une comparaison de leurs chances de survie," in Serge Jaumain, ed., *La réforme de l'État … et après? L'impact des débats institutionnels en Belgique et au Canada* (Brussels: Éditions de l'Université Libre de Bruxelles, 1997), 152. Author's translation. Stéphane Dion sees Pierre Elliott Trudeau as the father of this strategy.

19 Guy Laforest argues that "in the affair concerning Quebec's right of veto, the federal government has attempted to influence, if not intimidate deliberately, tribunals. In the winter of 1982, Buckingham Palace officially announced that the Queen would be visiting Canada to take part in the ceremony of ratification of the Constitutional Act. Preparations were under way even before the Quebec Court of Appeal had rendered its decision on 7 May 1982 on the question of Quebec's well-established right of veto." Guy Laforest, *Pour la liberté d'une société distinct: Parcours d'un intellectuel engagé* (Quebec: Les Presses de l'Université Laval, 2004), 130. Author's translation.

20 Gagnon and Segal, eds, *The Canadian Social Union*, chapters by Alain Noël, André Tremblay, and Claude Ryan.

21 Turp, *La nation bâillonnée.*

22 See Alberta and Quebec's opposition to this project, La Presse canadienne, "Valeurs mobilières: D'autres provinces s'opposeraient au plan Flaherty," *Le Devoir*, 15 June 2010.

23 These practices were subsequently investigated during the Gomery inquiry; see Brian O'Neal, Alex Smith, and Jack Stilborn (prepared by), "The Gomery Commission Report Phase 2," Library of Parliament, 16 February 2006. http://www.parl.gc.ca/Content/LOP/ResearchPub lications/prb0560-e.htm.

24 Jeremy Webber, *Reimagining Canada: Language, Culture, Community, and the Canadian Constitution* (Montreal: McGill-Queen's University Press, 1994), 229–59.

25 Claude Morin, *Le pouvoir québécois en négociation* (Montreal: Les Éditions du Boréal Express, 1972).

26 Frédéric Bastien, *Le poids de la coopération* (Montreal: Québec Amérique, Débats collection, 2006).

27 Montpetit, *Le fédéralisme d'ouverture*.

28 Dimitrios Karmis and Alain-G. Gagnon, "Federalism, Federation and Collective Identities in Canada and Belgium: Different Routes, Similar Fragmentation," in Gagnon and Tully, eds, *Multinational Democracies*, 137–75.

29 From Eddie Goldenberg, *Comment ça marche à Ottawa* (Montreal: Fides, 2007), 391–2, cited in Réjean Pelletier, *Le Québec et le fédéralisme canadien: Un regard critique* (Quebec: Les Presses de l'Université Laval, 2008), 230. Author's translation and emphasis.

30 See James Bickerton, "Janus Faces, Rocks, and Hard Places: Majority Nationalism in Canada," in Gagnon, Lecours, and Nootens, eds, *Contemporary Majority Nationalism*, pp. 144–80.

31 See Michael Burgess and Alain-G. Gagnon, "Introduction: Federalism and Democracy," in *Federal Democracies* (London: Routledge, 2010), 1–25. Also, Xabier Ezeizabarrena, *La ciaboga infinita: Una vision politica y juridica del conflicto vasco* (Irun: Alga, 2005).

32 Reference regarding the secession of Québec, [1998] 2 R.C.S. 217.

33 Within this context, the works of Daniel Elazar on federalism in complex societies are of paramount importance. See Elazar, *Exploring Federalism*; Jan Erk, *Explaining Federalism: State, Society and Congruence in Austria, Belgium, Canada, Germany and Switzerland* (London: Routledge, 2008); and Alain-G. Gagnon and Michael Keating, eds, *Political Autonomy and Divided Societies* (Basingstoke: Palgrave Macmillan, 2012).

34 Gagnon and Segal, eds, *The Canadian Social Union*; and Will Kymlicka, "Misunderstanding Nationalism," *Dissent* (Winter 1995), 130–7.

35 For more on the federal culture see Michael Burgess, *Comparative Federalism: Theory and Practice* (London: Routledge, 2006).

36 Morin, *Le pouvoir québécois en négociation.*
37 Philip Resnick and Daniel Latouche, *Letters to a Québécois Friend* (Montreal: McGill-Queen's University Press, 1990).
38 Gagnon and Lachapelle, "Québec Confronts Canada," 177–91.
39 Alain-G. Gagnon and Raffaele Iacovino, "Forget Gomery," *Globe and Mail*, 2 November 2005, A23.
40 Stephen Harper had this to say about an opposition coalition in December 2008: "This deal that the leader of the Liberal party has made with the separatists is a betrayal of the voters of this country, a betrayal of the best interests of our economy, a betrayal of the best interests of our country, and we will fight it with every means we have." http://www.canada.com/sas katoonstarphoenix/story.html?id=57301beb-48f0-407f-9134-2ea81cc46b4b. See also Alec Castonguay and Hélène Buzzetti, "Harper lance la contre-attaque," *Le Devoir*, 3 December 2008, A1. Castonguay and Buzzetti state that Harper characterized members of the Bloc Québécois as black sheep.
41 Pelletier, *Le Québec et le fédéralisme canadien*, 156–67.
42 Alec Castonguay and Antoine Robitaille, "Vingt ans après Meech: Le long hiver politique québécois," *Le Devoir*, 19–20 June 2010, A10. Michel David, "Une tragique pantalonnade," *Le Devoir*, 4 December 2008, A3.
43 Donald Smiley and Ronald L. Watts, *Intrastate Federalism in Canada*, vol. 39, Research Studies, Royal Commission on the Economic Union and Development Prospects for Canada (Macdonald commission) (Ottawa: Government Publishing Centre, Supply and Services Canada, 1985).
44 Robert Dahl and Charles E. Lindblom, *Politics, Economics, and Welfare* (New York: Harper, 1976 [1953]).
45 Robert Dahl, *Democracy and Its Critics* (New Haven: Yale University Press, 1989); Robert Dahl, *On Democracy* (New Haven: Yale University Press, 1998).
46 Reginald Whitaker, *A Sovereign Idea: Essays on Canada as a Democratic Community* (Montreal: McGill-Queen's University Press, 1992).
47 See Ramón Máiz, "Nation and Deliberation," in *The Inner Frontier: The Place of Nation in the Political Theory of Democracy and Federalism* (Brussels: Peter Lang, Diversitas collection, 2012), 135–74.
48 Presse canadienne, "Conseil de la Fédération: Les premiers ministres ne s'entendent pas sur tout," 6 August 2010. http://www.lapresse.ca/actual ites/quebec-canada/politique-canadienne/201008/06/01-4304582-conseil-de-la-federation-les-premiers-ministres-ne-sentendent-pas-sur-tout.php.
49 See Stéphane Paquin, ed., *Les relations internationales du Québec depuis la doctrine Gérin-Lajoie* (Quebec: Les Presses de l'Université Laval, 2006).
50 See Webber, *Reimagining Canada.*

51 Ferran Requejo, "Cultural Pluralism, Nationalism, and Federalism. A Revision of Democratic Citizenship in Plurinational States," *European Journal of Political Research* 35, no. 2 (1999) 255–86.
52 Peter Russell, "Trust and Distrust in Canada's Multinational Constitutional Politics," workshop, Groupe de recherche sur les sociétés plurinationales, 4 June 2010.
53 The Québécois response has changed very little since Charest's election in 2003. See Gagnon, *The Case for Multinational Federalism*, chapter 4.
54 See Seymour and Royer, "Les nations comme sujets," in Seymour, ed., *La reconnaissance*, 157–84.
55 Michel Seymour, *De la tolérance à la reconnaissance* (Montreal: Boréal, 2008); Seymour, ed., *La reconnaissance dans tous ses états*.
56 Alain-G. Gagnon, "Le Québec, une nation inscrite au sein d'une démocratie étriquée," in Alan-G. Gagnon and Jocelyn Maclure, eds, *Repères en mutation: Identité et citoyenneté dane le Québec contemporain* (Montreal: Québec Amérique, Débats collection, 2001), 37–65.
57 Such a project benefits from James Tully's work in *Public Philosophy in a New Key*, vol. 1, *Democracy and Civic Freedom*, as well as vol. 2, *Imperialism and Civic Freedom* (Cambridge: Cambridge University Press, 2008).
58 James Tully, "The Struggles of Indigenous Peoples for and of Freedom," in P. Patton, D. Ivison, and D. Saunders, eds, *Political Theory and Indigenous Rights* (Cambridge: Cambridge University Press, 2000), 36–59.
59 For an excellent text on nation building in Canada, see Claude Ryan, "Nation-Building in a Multinational Society: The Canadian Experience since World War II," presented at the British Association of Canadian Studies Conference, University of Edinburgh, 12 April 2000.

5. Towards Multinational Federalism

1 *The Rights Revolution* (Toronto: Anansi, 2000), 84.
2 In Québec, the notion of consociationalism has not received much attention from researchers and politicians. However, there is an important exception to this in the study by Garth Stevenson, *Parallel Paths* (Montreal: McGill-Queen's University Press, 2006), but that is one of the rare pieces of research that has used this analytic framework.
3 Cases in point can be found in many countries, including China and Thailand. See Isabelle Côté, "Autonomy and Ethnic Diversity: The Case of Xinjiang Uighur Autonomous Region in China," and Jacques Bertrand, "Autonomy and Nationalist Demands in Southeast Asia," in Gagnon and Keating, eds, *Political Autonomy and Divided Societies*, 171–84 and 200–19.

4 Will Kymlicka, *Multicultural Odysseys: Navigating in the New International Politics of Diversity* (Oxford: Oxford University Press, 2007).

5 Will Kymlicka, "Rights to Culture, Autonomy and Participation: The Evolving Basis of International Norms of Minority Rights," in John McGarry and Michael Keating, eds, *Nations, Minorities and European Integration* (London: Routledge, 2006), 35–63.

6 Conference on Security and Co-operation in Europe, *Document of the Copenhagen Meeting of the Conference on the Human Dimension of the CSCE* (Copenhagen: Organization for Security and Co-operation in Europe, 1990), para. 35. Council of Europe, *Framework Convention for the Protection of National Minorities* (Strasbourg: Council of Europe, 1995). http://conventions.coe.int/Treaty/en/Treaties/Html/157.htm.

7 Council of Europe, *Framework Convention for the Protection of National Minorities.* http://conventions.coe.int/Treaty/en/Treaties/Html/157.htm.

8 Concerning the distinction between governmental autonomy and good governance, see Francesco Palermo, "When the Lund Recommendations Are Ignored: Effective Participation of National Minorities through Territorial Autonomy," *International Journal on Minority and Group Rights* 16, no. 4 (2009), 1–11.

9 Yet some authors, such as Sabine Riedel, see the notion of "minority" as applying only to national minorities. See "Minorités nationales en Europe et protection des droits de l'homme: Un enjeu pour l'élargissement," *Politique étrangère* 3 (2002), 653.

10 Venice Commission, *Opinion on the Interpretation of Article 11 of the Draft Protocol to the European Convention on Human Rights Appended to Recommendation 1201 of the Parliamentary Assembly* (Venice: Council of Europe, 1996). Accessed 6 December 2012. http://www.venice.coe.int/docs/1996/CDL-INF(1996)004-E.asp?MenuL=E.

11 Heinrich Klebes, "Projet de protocole additionnel de l'Assemblée parlementaire à la Convention européenne pour la protection des minorités nationales," *Revue universelle des droits de l'homme* 5, nos. 5–6 (1993), 183–7.

12 Sujit Choudhry, "Bridging Comparative Politics and Comparative Political Law: Constitutional Design in Divided Societies," in S. Choudhry, ed., *Constitutional Design for Divided Societies: Integration or Accommodation?* (Oxford: Oxford University Press), 14.

13 Arend Lijphart, *Democracy in Plural Societies: A Comparative Exploration* (New Haven: Yale University Press, 1977), 24.

14 Guy Laforest, *De la prudence* (Montreal: Boréal, 1993).

15 On this theme, see also André Lecours and Geneviève Nootens, eds, *Dominant Nationalism, Dominant Ethnicity: Identity, Federalism and Democracy*

(Brussels: Les Presses interuniversitaires européennes/Peter Lang, 2009); Gagnon, Lecours, and Nootens, eds, *Contemporary Majority Nationalism*; and Dimitrios Karmis and François Rocher, eds, *La dynamique confiance/ méfiance dans les démocraties multinationales: Sous l'angle comparatif* (Quebec: Les Presses de l'Université Laval, 2012).

16 Brendan O'Leary, "An Iron's Law of Nationalism and Federation? A (Neo-Diceyan) Theory of the Necessity of a Federal Staatsvolk, and a Constitutional Rescue," *Nations and Nationalism* 7, no. 3 (2001), 273–96.

17 Ian Lustick, "Stability in Deeply-Divided Societies: Consociationalism versus Control," *World Politics* 31, no. 3 (1979), 325–44.

18 Milton Esman describes institutionalized domination as one of the four possible means of managing community conflicts. The other three are forced assimilation, syncretic integration, and balanced pluralism. See "The Management of Communal Conflict," *Public Policy* 21, no. 1 (1973), 49–78.

19 Tully, *Strange Multiplicity*; see also Tully's introductory chapter to Gagnon and Tully, eds, *Multinational Democracies*.

20 Gagnon and Iacovino, *Federalism, Citizenship, and Quebec*.

21 Michael Burgess, "From Dominance to Partnership: The Inheritance of Majority Nations in Multinational Federations," in A. Lecours and G. Nootens, eds, *Dominant Nationalism, Dominant Ethnicity*, 173–91.

22 Turp, *La nation bâillonnée*.

23 Since then, the book has been released in Catalan, English, and Spanish, and an abridged German edition has been published in 2011.

24 For immigration policies in Catalonia, Flanders, and Quebec, see Zapata-Barrero, ed., *Immigration and Self-Government of Minority Nations*.

25 Palermo, "When the Lund Recommendations Are Ignored."

26 See Hurst Hannum, "The Right to Autonomy: Chimera or Solution," in K. Rupesinghe and V.A. Tishkov, eds, *Ethnicity and Power in the Contemporary World* (Tokyo: United Nations University Press, 1996); Hannum, "The Limits of Sovereignty and Majority Rule: Minorities, Indigenous Peoples and the Right to Autonomy," in E. Lutz, H. Hannum, and K.J. Burke, eds, *New Directions in Human Rights* (Philadelphia: University of Pennsylvania Press, 1989), 3–24; Zelim Skurbaty, *Beyond a One-Dimensional State: An Emerging Right to Autonomy?* (Leiden: Martinus Nijhoff, 2008); and Daniel Turp, "Le droit à la sécession: L'expression du principe démocratique," in Alain-G. Gagnon and François Rocher, eds, *Répliques aux détracteurs de la souveraineté du Québec* (Montreal: VLB éditeur 1992), 49–55. See also Jacques-Yvan Morin and José Woehrling, *Demain, le Québec: Choix politiques et constitutionnels d'un pays en devenir* (Quebec: Septentrion, 1994), in which

the authors go into great detail on Quebec gaining sovereignty without the agreement of English Canada with a unilateral secession.

27 See Brouillet, *Négation de la nation*.
28 Alan Patten, "Beyond the Dichotomy of Universalism and Difference: Four Response to Cultural Diversity," and Kymlicka, "Internationalization of Minority," in Choudhry, ed., *Constitutional Design*, 91–110 and 111–40.
29 John Packer, "Autonomy within the OSCE: The Case of Crimea," in M. Suksi, ed., *Autonomy, Applications and Implications* (La Haye: Kluwer, 1998), 295–316.

6. Rethinking Intercommunal Relations in Canada

1 Ferran Requejo, *Multinational Federalism and Value Pluralism: The Spanish Case* (London: Routledge, 2005), 50.
2 Guy Laforest and Roger Gibbins, eds, *Beyond the Impasse, Toward Reconciliation* (Montreal: Institute for Research on Public Policy, 1998).
3 Will Kymlicka, "Multinational Federalism," in Laforest and Gibbins, eds, *Beyond the Impasse*, 16.
4 David Schneiderman, "Human Rights, Fundamental Differences? Multiple Charters in a Partnership Frame," in Laforest and Gibbins, eds, *Beyond the Impasse*, 148.
5 Jane Jenson, "Recognising Difference: Distinct Societies, Citizenship Regime and Partnership," in Laforest and R. Gibbins, eds, *Beyond the Impasse*, 215.
6 Or, in Kant's words: "There is nothing more natural than ... to put ourselves in thought in the place of everyone else." Immanuel Kant, *Critique of Judgment* (New York: Hafner Publishing Co., 1951), 136; author's translation. See Guy Laforest, "Standing in the Shoes of the Other Partners in the Canadian Union," in Laforest and Gibbins, eds, *Beyond the Impasse*, 75.
7 John Kincaid, "Introduction to the Handbook of Federal Countries," Forum of Federations. See http://www.forumfed.org/en/federalism/introductiontohandbook.php.
8 François Rocher et Benoît Pelletier, eds, *Le nouvel ordre constitutionnel canadien: Du raptriement de 1982 à nos jours* (Quebec: Les Presses de l'Université du Québec, Politeia collection, 2013).
9 Jean Pierre Barraqué, "Pactisme et pactismes," *Sciences de l'Homme et de la Société*, 25 June 2008, 2.
10 Ibid.
11 Francesc Eiximenis, Dotzè del Crestia, chapter 603, quoted in Barraqué, ibid.

12 Tzvetan Todorov, *In Defense of the Enlightenment* (London: Atlantic Books, 2009).
13 See Maria Isabel Wences Simon, *Sociedad civil y virtud civica en Adam Fergu-son* (Madrid: Centro de Estudios Politicos y Constitucionales, 2006), chapter 6. See also Norbert Waszek, *L'Écosse des Lumières: Hume, Smith, Ferguson* (Paris: Les Presses universitaires de France, 2003).
14 S. Rufus Davis, *The Federal Principle: A Journey through Time in Quest of Meaning* (London: University of California Press, 1978).
15 Michael Burgess, "The Federal Spirit as a Moral Basis to Canadian Federalism," *International Journal of Canadian Studies*, no. 22, Fall (2000), 13–35.
16 Miquel Caminal, *El federalismo pluralista: Del federalismo nacional al federalismo plurinacional* (Barcelona: Paidos, 2002), 74–105; Requejo, *Multinational Federalism*, chapter 3.
17 Research in this area has focused primarily on public opinion. See Patrick Fafard, François Rocher, and Catherine Côté, "The Presence (or Lack Thereof) of a Federal Culture in Canada," *Regional and Federal Studies* 20, no. 1 (2010), 19–43, and Richard L. Cole and John Kincaid, "Public Opinion on Federalism and Federal Political Culture in Canada, Mexico, and the United States, 2004," *Publius: The Journal of Federalism* 34, no. 3 (2004), 201–21.
18 Ivo D. Duchacek, *Comparative Federalism: The Territorial Dimension of Politics* (New York: University Press of America, 1987), 346.
19 Elazar, *Exploring Federalism*, 192.
20 Samuel V. LaSelva, *The Moral Foundations of Canadian Federalism: Paradoxes, Achievements, and Tragedies of Nationhood* (Montreal: McGill-Queen's University Press, 1996).
21 See Alain-G. Gagnon, "The Moral Foundations of Asymmetrical Federalism: A Normative Exploration of the Case of Quebec and Canada," in Gagnon and Tully, eds, *Multinational Democracies*, 319–38; and François Rocher, "Fédéralisme canadien et culture(s) publique(s) commune(s): le casse-tête du pluralisme identitaire," in Gervais, Karmis, and Lamoureux, eds, *Du tricoté serré*, 141–63.
22 Dimitrios Karmis, "The Multiple Voices," in Gagnon, ed., *Contemporary Canadian Federalism*, 68–9.
23 Ronald Watts, "Federalism and Diversity in Canada," in Y. Ghai, ed., *Autonomy and Ethnicity: Negotiating Competing Claims in Multi-Ethnic States* (Cambridge: Cambridge University Press, 2000), 49. See also Ronald Watts, *Comparing Federal Systems* (Montreal: McGill-Queen's University Press, 2008).

24 See Dimitrios Karmis and Jocelyn Maclure, "Two Escape Routes from the Paradigm of Monistic Authenticity: Post-Imperialist and Federal Perspectives on Plural and Complex Identities," *Ethnic and Racial Studies* 24, no. 3 (2001), 361–85. See also Gagnon, *The Case for Multinational Federalism*.

25 Michael Burgess, "Managing Diversity in Federal States: Conceptual Lenses and Comparative Perspectives," in Gagnon, ed., *Contemporary Canadian Federalism*, 431–2.

26 Requejo, *Multinational Federalism and Value Pluralism*; Carles Viver, "Una deriva peligrosa del Tribunal Constitucional," *La Vanguardia*, 10 May 2010.

27 Raoul Blindenbacher and Ronald Watts, "Federalism in a Changing World – A Conceptual Framework for the Conference," in R. Blindenbacher and A. Koller, eds, *Federalism in a Changing World: Learning from Each Other* (Montreal: McGill-Queen's University Press, 2002), 11.

28 See Jean-François Caron, Guy Laforest, and Catherine Vallières-Roland, "Canada's Federative Deficit," in Gagnon, ed., *Contemporary Canadian Federalism*, 134–5.

29 Ibid., 150.

30 Joan Romero Gonzalez, "Autonomia politica y acomodo de la diversidad en Espana," in J. Arrieta and J. Astigarraga, eds, *Conciliar la diversidad: Pasado y presente de la vertebracion de Espana* (Bilbao: Universidad del Pais Vasco, 2009), 161–89.

31 See Robert A. Williams, Jr, *Linking Arms Together: American Indian Treaty Vision of Law and Peace, 1600–1800* (London: Routledge, 1999); and Martin Papillon, "Towards Postcolonial Federalism? The Challenges of Aboriginal Self-Determination in the Canadian Context," in Gagnon, ed., *Contemporary Canadian Federalism*, 463.

32 Tully, *Strange Multiplicity*, 140.

33 See Bruce H. Wildsmith, "Treaty Responsibilities: A Co-Relational Model," *University of British Columbia Law Review* 26 (1992), 324–37; James Tully, "Aboriginal Peoples: Negotiating Reconciliation," in A.-G. Gagnon and J. Bickerton, eds, *Canadian Politics*, 3rd ed. (Toronto: University of Toronto Press, 1999), 411–39; James (Sa'ke'j) Youngblood Henderson, "Treaty Governance," in Y.D. Belanger, ed., *Aboriginal Self-government in Canada* (Saskatoon: Purich Publishing, 2008); and James R. Miller, *Compact, Contract, Covenant: Aboriginal Treaty-Making in Canada* (Toronto: University of Toronto Press, 2009).

34 James Tully, "The Struggles of Indigenous Peoples for and of Freedom," in P. Patton, D. Ivison, and D. Saunders, eds, *Political Theory and Indigenous Rights* (Cambridge: Cambridge University Press, 2000), 41.

35 The new statute of autonomy being adhered to (and later diminished) in Catalonia confirms this interpretation.

36 Tully, "The Struggles of Indigenous Peoples," 53.

37 Ibid.

38 This is well documented in Miller, *Compact, Contract, Covenant*, 283–309.

39 Royal Commission on Aboriginal Peoples (Erasmus-Dussault), *Final Report. Restructuring the Relationship*, vol. 2, part 1 (Ottawa: Groupe Communications Canada, 1996). http://www.collectionscanada.gc.ca/webarchives/2007 1124125001/http://www.ainc-inac.gc.ca/ch/rcap/sg/sh1_e.html.

40 Ibid. See also the works of Sakej Henderson, such as "Empowering Treaty Federalism," *Saskatchewan Law Review* 58, no. 2 (1994), 271–315, as well as Taiaiake Alfred, *Peace, Power and Righteousness: An Indigenous Manifesto* (Toronto: Oxford University Press, 1994) and Thomas Hueglin, "From Constitutional to Treaty Federalism: A Comparative Perspective," *Publius* 30, no. 4 (2000), 137–63.

41 Sébastien Grammond, *Aménager la coexistence: Les peuples autochtones et le droit canadien* (Brussels/Montreal: Bruylant/Éditions Yvon Blais, 2003), 106.

42 *R. v. Van der Peet*, 2 SCR 507, the Chief Justice Antonio Lamer, section V, para. 30.

43 See Thomas Flanagan, *First Nations? Second Thoughts* (Montreal: McGill-Queen's University Press, 2000).This book won the Donner Foundation's book of the year prize and was also awarded a prestigious prize at the annual meeting of the Canadian Political Science Association. One should also read Frances Widdowson and Albert Howard, *Disrobing the Aboriginal Industry: The Deception behind Indigenous Cultural Preservation* (Montreal: McGill-Queen's University Press, 2008), which launches a full-scale assault on indigenous claims making.

44 Salée, "Enjeux et défis," 139–61.

45 Christophe Parent, *Le concept d'état fédéral multinational: Essai sur l'union des peuples* (Brussels: Les Presses interuniversitaires européennes/Peter Lang, Diversitas collection, 2011), 498.

46 Miller, *Compact, Contract, Covenant*, 306.

Conclusion

1 *The Plural States of Recognition* (Basingstoke: Palgrave Macmillan, 2010) 162.

2 See also Alain Renaut, who devotes several pages to this same topic in *Un humanisme de la diversité: Essai sur la décolonisation des identités* (Paris: Flammarion, 2009), 285–96.

3 See Lluis Bonet and Emmanuel Négrier, eds, *La fin des cultures nationales? Les politiques culturelles à l'épreuve de la diversité* (Grenoble: La Découverte/ Pacte, 2008).

4 Sakiko Fukuda-Parr, *Cultural Liberty in Today's Diverse World*, Human Development Report 2004 (New York: United Nations Development Programme, 2004).

5 Renaut, *Un humanisme de la diversité*, 288. Author's translation.

6 John Emerich Acton, "Nationality," in G. Himmelfarb, ed., *Essays on Freedom and Power* (Glencoe: The Free Press, 1949), 185.

7 For more on liberal communitarianism, see Kymlicka, *Multicultural Citizenship*.

8 Eugénie Brouillet, *Négation de la nation: L'identité culturelle québécoise et le fédéralisme canadien* (Quebec: Septentrion, 2005); Michel Seymour, *Le pari de la démesure: L'intransigeance canadienne face au Québec* (Montreal: L'Hexagone, 2001).

9 Renaut, *Un humanisme de la diversité*, 73. Author's translation.

10 By taking advantage of a movement opposed to constitutional asymmetry, several autonomous regions (Andalusia, Aragon, and the Balearic Islands) have been able to acquire a statute of historical nationality over the last few years. The Canary Islands have also put in a claim for formal recognition.

11 Within this context, we can also note a significant thawing of the heretofore icy relationship between civil society and the Spanish intelligentsia. See the following articles: Enric Juliana, "El respeto," *La Vanguardia*, 28 November 2009, 15; Pablo Salvador Coderch, "Estrategia del reencuentro," *El Pais*, 28 November 2009, 31; Carles Viver i Pi-Sunyer, "Una deriva peligrosa del Tribunal Constitucional," *La Vanguardia*, 10 May 2010; Ferran Requejo, "Hacia la independencia," *La Vanguardia*, 7 June 2010; Salvador Cardus i Ros, "Ilusion i compromiso," *La Vanguardia*, 7 July 2010, 22; Miquel Caminal, "De sabios es rectificar," *El Pais*, 12 July 2010, 29–30.

12 Rajeev Bhargava, "Hegel, Taylor and the Phenomenology of Broken Spirits," in Seymour, ed., *The Plural States of Recognition* (Basingstoke: Palgrave Macmillan, 2010), 39.

13 Daniel Innerarity, *Éthique de l'hospitalité* (Quebec: Les Presses de l'Université Laval, 2009).

14 Ibid., 4. Author's translation.

15 The Bouchard-Taylor commission's report on practices of cultural and religious accommodation highlights many of these factors. See Bouchard and Taylor, *Building the Future*.

16 Manuel Castells, *The Power of Identity* (Malden: Blackwell Publishing, 1997).

17 See the special edition of *Quaderns de la Mediterrania*, "Los retos de la inter-culturalidad en el Mediterraneo," Institut catala de la Mediterrania, no. 1 (2000); and Gérard Bouchard, *L'interculturalisme: Un point de vue québécois* (Montreal: Boréal, 2012).
18 Daniel Innerarity, *The Transformation of Politics: Governing in the Age of Complex Societies* (Brussels: Peter Lang, Diversitas collection, 2010), p. 79.

Bibliography

Abu-Laban, Yasmeen, and Daiva Stasiulis. "Ethnic Pluralism Under Siege: Popular and Partisan Opposition to Multiculturalism." *Canadian Public Policy* 18, no. 4 (1992), 365–86.

Ajzenstat, Janet, et al. *Débats sur la fondation du Canada.* French edition commented on and edited by Stéphane Kelly and Guy Laforest. Quebec: Les Presses de l'Université Laval, 2004.

Alesina, Alberto, and Enrico Spolaore. *The Size of Nations.* Cambridge, MA: MIT Press, 2003.

Alfred, Taiaiake. *Peace, Power and Righteousness: An Indigenous Manifesto.* Toronto: Oxford University Press, 1994.

Arbos, Xavier, ed. *L'abast de l'autonomia politica del Quebec.* Barcelona: Parlament de Catalunya, 2006.

Arrieta, Jon, and Jesus Astigarraga, eds. *Conciliar la diversidad: Pasado y presente de la vertebracion de Espana.* Bilbao: Universidad del Pais Vasco, 2009.

Azzam, Simone, and Marie Mc Andrew. *Évaluation des services offerts dans le cadre du PELO et de l'impact de ce programme sur les élèves et les écoles à la CECM.* Research study. Montreal: Commission des écoles catholiques de Montréal, 1987.

Barraqué, Jean Pierre. "Pactisme et pactismes." *Sciences de l'Homme et de la Société*, 25 June 2008.

Bastien, Frédéric. *Le poids de la coopération.* Montreal: Québec Amérique, Débats collection, 2006.

Beauchemin, Jacques, Gilles Bourque, and Jules Duchastel. "Du providentialisme au néolibéralisme: De Marsh à Axworthy. Un nouveau discours de légitimation de la régulation sociale." *Cahiers de recherche sociologique* 24 (1995).

Beaud, Olivier. *Théorie de la federation*. Paris: Les Presses universitaires de France, 2009.

Belanger, Yale D., ed. *Aboriginal Self-government in Canada: Current Trends and Issues*. Saskatoon: Purich Publishing, 2008.

Belliveau, Joel, and Frédéric Boily. "Deux révolutions tranquilles? Transformations politiques et sociales au Québec et au Nouveau-Brunswick (1960–1967)." *Recherches sociographiques* 46, no. 1 (2005), 11–34.

Bendix, Reinhart. *Nation-Building and Citizenship*. Berkeley: University of California Press, 1964.

Bennett, Andrew, and Wallace Peter. *Nations of Distinction: An Analysis of Nationalist Perspectives on Constitutional Change in Québec, Catalunya, and Scotland*. Doctoral dissertation, University of Edinburgh, 2001.

Bergeron, Gérard. *Notre miroir à deux faces, Trudeau, Lévesque … et forcément avec bien d'autres*. Montreal: Québec Amérique, 1985.

Berlin, Isaiah. "Two Concepts of Liberty." In Henry Hardy, ed., *Liberty*. Oxford: Oxford University Press, 2002.

Bissoondath, Neil. *Selling Illusions: The Cult of Multiculturalism in Canada*. Toronto: Penguin Books, 1994.

Blindenbacher, Raoul, and Arnold Koller, eds. *Federalism in a Changing World: Learning from Each Other*. Montreal: McGill-Queen's University Press, 2002.

Bofill, Hector. *La Democràcia Cuirassada*. Barcelone: Esfera des llibres, 2005.

Bonet, Lluis, and Emmanuel Négrier, eds. *La fin des cultures nationales? Les politiques culturelles à l'épreuve de la diversité*. Grenoble: La Découverte/Pacte, 2008.

Bouchard, Gérard. *L'interculturalisme: Un point de vue québécois*. Montreal: Boréal, 2012.

Bouchard, Gérard, and Charles Taylor. *Building the Future: A Time for Reconciliation*. Quebec: Gouvernement du Québec, 2008.

Boucher, Jacques L., and Joseph Yvon Thériault, eds. *Petites sociétés et minorités nationales: Enjeux politiques et perspectives compares*. Quebec: Les Presses de l'Université du Québec, 2005.

Brooks, Stephen, ed. *The Challenge of Cultural Pluralism*. Westport, CT: Praeger, 2002.

Brouillet, Eugénie. *La négation de la nation: L'identité culturelle québécoise et le fédéralisme canadien*. Quebec: Septentrion, 2005.

Brubaker, Rogers. *Citizenship and Nationhood in France and Germany*. Cambridge, MA: Harvard University Press, 1992.

Burelle, André. *Le droit à la différence à l'heure de la globalisation: Le cas du Québec et du Canada*. Montreal: Fides, 1996.

Burgess, Michael. *Comparative Federalism: Theory and Practice*. London: Routledge, 2006.

Burgess, Michael. "The Federal Spirit as a Moral Basis to Canadian Federalism." *International Journal of Canadian Studies* 22 (Fall 2000), 13–35.

Burgess, Michael, and Alain-G. Gagnon, eds. *Federal Democracies*. London: Routledge, 2010.

Calhoun, Craig. *Cosmopolitanism and Belonging*. Abington, Oxford: Routledge, 1992.

Calhoun, Craig. *Nations Matter: Culture, History, and the Cosmopolitan Dream*. London: Routledge, 2007.

Cameron, David R., and Janice Gross Stein. "L'État, un lieu parmi les espaces en transformation." In *Contestation et mondialisation: Repenser la culture et la communication*. Montreal: Les Presses de l'Université de Montréal, 2003.

Cameron, David R., and Janice Gross Stein, eds. *Street Protest and Fantasy Parks*. Vancouver: UBC Press, 2002.

Caminal, Miquel. "De sabios es rectificar." *El Pais*, 12 July 2010, 29–30.

Caminal, Miquel i Badia. *El federalismo pluralista: Del federalismo nacional al federalismo plurinacional*. Barcelone: Paidos, 2002.

Caminal, Miquel, and Ferran Requejo, eds. *Federalisme i plurinacionalitat: Teoria i anàlisi de casos*. Barcelona: Institut d'Estudis Autonomics, Classics del Federalisme collection, 2009.

Cardinal, Linda, ed. *Le fédéralisme asymétrique et les minorités linguistiques et nationales*. Sudbury: Éditions Prise de parole, 2008.

Cardús i Ros, Salvador. "Ilusion i compromise." *La Vanguardia*, 7 July 2010, 22.

Carens, Joseph. *Culture, Citizenship and Community: Contextual Exploration of Justice as Evenhandedness*. Oxford: Oxford University Press, 2000.

Caron, Jean-François. "L'héritage républicain du fédéralisme: une théorie de l'identité nationale dans les fédérations multinationals." *Politique et Sociétés* 25, nos. 2–3 (2006), 121–46.

Casajuana, Carles. *Le dernier homme qui parlait catalan*. Paris: Robert Laffont, 2009.

Castellà Andreu, Josep Ma I, and Sébastien Grammond, eds. *Diversidad, derechos fundamentals y federalismo: Un dialogo entre Canada y Espana*. Barcelona: Libros juridicos, 2010.

Castells, Manuel. *The Power of Identity*. Malden: Blackwell Publishing, 1997.

Castonguay, Alec, and Hélène Buzzetti. "Harper lance la contre-attaque." *Le Devoir*, 3 December 2008, A1.

Castonguay, Alec, and Antoine Robitaille. "Vingt ans après Meech: Le long hiver politique québécois." *Le Devoir*, 19–20 June 2010, A10.

Catalan, Language of Europe. Barcelona: Generalitat de Catalunya, Departament de la Vicepresidència, Secretaria de Política Lingüística. http://www20. gencat.cat/docs/Llengcat/Documents/Publicacions/Catala%20llengua%20 Europa/Arxius/cat_europa_angles_07.pdf.

Chevrette, François, and Herbert Marx. *Droit constitutionnel*. Montreal: Les Presses de l'Université de Montréal, 1982.

Chevrier, Marc. "La démocratie, ses empires et le Dominion multiculturel canadien." *Médiane* 3, no. 2 (2008).

Choudhry, Sujit, ed. *Constitutional Design for Divided Societies: Integration or Accommodation?* Oxford: Oxford University Press, 2008.

Coderch, Pablo Salvador. "Estrategia del reencuentro." *El Pais*, 28 November 2009, 31.

Cole, Richard L., and John Kincaid. "Public Opinion on Federalism and Federal Political Culture in Canada, Mexico, and the United States, 2004." *Publius: The Journal of Federalism* 34, no. 3 (2004), 201–21.

Conference on Security and Co-operation in Europe. *Document of the Copenhagen Meeting of the Conference on the Human Dimension of the CSCE*. Copenhagen: Organization for Security and Co-operation in Europe, 1990.

Consolidation of Inuit Language Protection Act (2008). http://langcom.nu.ca/ sites/langcom.nu.ca/files/consSNu2008c17.pdf.

Conway, John F. *Debts to Pay: The Future of Canadian Federalism in Quebec*. 3rd edition. Toronto: James Lorimer, 2004.

Corbeil, Jean-Claude. *De l'embarras des langues: Origine, conception, évolution de la politique linguistique québécoise*. Montreal: Québec Amérique, 2008.

Coughlin, James T. "Lobbying for Language: Alliance Québec, the Société des Acadiens du Nouveau-Brunswick and Federal Conciliation in Minority Language Rights." Honours essay, Department of Political Science, Carleton University, Ottawa, 1986.

Council of Europe. *White Paper on Intercultural Dialogue: Living Together as Equals in Dignity*. Strasburg, Council of Europe, 2008. http://www.coe. int/t/dg4/intercultural/source/white%20paper_final_revised_en.pdf.

Council of Europe. *Framework Convention for the Protection of National Minorities*. Strasbourg: Council of Europe, 1995.

Cyr, Hugo. *Canadian Federalism and Treaty Powers: Organic Constitutionalism at Work*. Brussels: Les Presses interuniversitaires européennes–Peter Lang, Diversitas collection, 2009.

Dahl, Robert. *Democracy and Its Critics*. New Haven: Yale University Press, 1989.

Dahl, Robert. *On Democracy*. New Haven: Yale University Press, 1998.

Dahl, Robert, and Charles E. Lindblom. *Politics, Economics, and Welfare*. New York: Harper, 1976 [1953].

Danspeckgruber, Wolgang, ed. *The Self-Determination of Peoples: Community, Nation, and State in an Interdependent World*. London: Lynne Rienner Publishers, 2002.

Dardanelli, Paolo. "Multinational Switzerland?" *Swiss Political Science Review* 14, no. 3 (2008), 551–77.

David, Michel. "Une sinistre farce." *Le Devoir*, 17 April 2008, A3.

David, Michel. "Une tragique pantalonnade." *Le Devoir*, 4 December 2008, A3.

Davis, S. Rufus. *The Federal Principle: A Journey through Time in Quest of Meaning*. Berkeley, CA, and London: University of California Press, 1978.

Deveaux, Monique. *Gender and Justice in Multicultural Liberal States*. Oxford: Oxford University Press, 2006.

Dickinson, John A., and Brian Young. *A Short History of Quebec*. Toronto: Copp Clark Pitman, 1993.

Dieckhoff, Alain. "L'état face au défi de la multinationalité." In Alain-G. Gagnon and Jocelyn Maclure, eds, *Repères en mutation: Identité et citoyenneté dans le Québec contemporain*. Montreal: Québec Amérique, Débats collection, 2001.

Dieckhoff, Alain, ed. *La constellation des appartenances: Nationalisme, libéralisme et pluralisme*. Paris: Les Presses de Sciences Po, 2004.

di Norcia, Vincent. "Le fédéralisme, l'État et la démocratie." *Philosophiques* 8, no. 1 (1981), 167–84.

Dorais, Louis-Jacques. "Discours et identité à Iqaluit après l'avènement du Nunavut." *Études Inuit* 30, no. 2 (2006), 163–89.

Duchacek, Ivo D. *Comparative Federalism: The Territorial Dimension of Politics*. New York: University Press of America, 1987.

Dutrisac, Robert. "Québec bafoue la Charte de la langue." *Le Devoir*, 17 April 2008, A1–8.

Elazar, Daniel J. *Exploring Federalism*. Tuscaloosa: University of Alabama Press, 1987.

Entente de coopération en matière linguistique entre le gouvernement du Québec et le gouvernement autonome de la Catalogne. Quebec: Ministère des Relations internationales, 1996.

Erk, Jan. *Explaining Federalism: State, Society and Congruence in Austria, Belgium, Canada, Germany and Switzerland*. London: Routledge, 2008.

Erk, Jan, and Alain-G. Gagnon. "Constitutional Ambiguity and Federal Trust: The Codification of Federalism in Belgium, Canada and Spain." *Regional and Federal Studies* 10, no. 1 (2000), 92–111.

Esman, Milton. "The Management of Communal Conflict." *Public Policy* 21, no. 1 (1973), 49–78.

Ezeizabarrena, Xabier. *La ciaboga infinita: Una vision politica y juridica del conflicto vasco*. Irun, Spain: Alga, 2005.

Fafard, Patrick, François Rocher, and Catherine Côté. "The Presence (or Lack Thereof) of a Federal Culture in Canada." *Regional and Federal Studies* 20, no. 1 (2010), 19–43.

Ferro, Marc, ed. *Le livre noir du colonialisme, XVe–XXIe siècle: De l'extermination à la repentance.* Paris: Robert Laffont, 2003.

Flanagan, Thomas. *First Nations? Second Thoughts.* Montreal: McGill-Queen's University Press, 2000.

Foley, Michael. *The Silence of Constitutions: Gaps, Abeyances and Political Temperament in the Maintenance of Governance.* London, New York: Routledge, 1989.

Forbes, Donald. "Immigration and Multiculturalism vs. Quebec Separatism: An Interpretation of Canadian Constitutional Politics since 1968." Paper presented at American Political Science Association annual meeting, Chicago, 30 August 2007.

Fossas, Enric, ed. *Les transformacions de la sobirania i el futur politic de Catalunya.* Barcelona: Proa, 2000.

Fraser, Graham. *Annual Report 2009–2010. Beyond Obligations.* Ottawa: Office of the Commissioner of Official Languages, Minister of Public Works and Government Services Canada, 2010. Vol. 1.

Fukuda-Parr, Sakiko. *Cultural Liberty in Today's Diverse World.* Human Development Report 2004. New York: United Nations Development Programme, 2004.

Gagnon, Alain-G. *The Case for Multinational Federalism: Beyond the All-Encompassing Nation.* London: Routledge, 2010.

Gagnon, Alain-G., ed. *Contemporary Canadian Federalism: Foundations, Traditions, Institutions.* Toronto: University of Toronto Press, 2009.

Gagnon, Alain-G., ed. *Quebec State and Society.* 3rd edition. Toronto: University of Toronto Press, 2004.

Gagnon, Alain-G., and James Bickerton, eds. *Canadian Politics.* 3rd edition. Peterborough: Broadview Press, 1999.

Gagnon, Alain-G., Montserrat Guibernau, and François Rocher, eds. *The Conditions of Diversity in Multinational Democracies.* Montreal: McGill-Queen's University Press, 2003.

Gagnon, Alain-G., and Raffaele Iacovino. *Federalism, Citizenship, and Quebec: Debating Multinationalism.* Toronto: University of Toronto Press, 2007.

Gagnon, Alain-G., and Michael Keating, eds. *Political Autonomy and Divided Societies.* Basingstoke: Palgrave Macmillan, 2012.

Gagnon, Alain-G., and Guy Lachapelle. "Québec Confronts Canada: Two Competing Societal Projects Searching for Legitimacy." *Publius* 26, no. 3 (1996), 177–91.

Gagnon, Alain-G., and Daniel Latouche. *Allaire, Bélanger, Campeau et les autres: Les Québécois face à leur avenir*. Montreal: Québec Amérique, 1991.

Gagnon, Alain-G., André Lecours, and Geneviève Nootens, eds. *Contemporary Majority Nationalism*. Montreal and Kingston: McGill-Queen's University Press, 2011.

Gagnon, Alain-G., and Jocelyn Maclure, eds. *Repères en mutation: Identité et citoyenneté dans le Québec contemporain*. Montreal: Québec Amérique, Débats collection, 2001.

Gagnon, Alain-G., and Alain Noël, eds. *L'espace québécois*. Montreal: Québec Amérique, 1995.

Gagnon, Alain-G., and François Rocher, eds. *Répliques aux détracteurs de la souveraineté du Québec*. Montreal: VLB éditeur, 1992.

Gagnon, Alain-G., and Hugh Segal, eds. *The Canadian Social Union: 8 Critical Analyses*. Montreal: McGill-Queen's University Press, 2000.

Gagnon, Alain-G., and Richard Simeon. "Unity and Diversity in Canada: A Preliminary Assessment." In Luis Moreno and César Colino Cámara, eds, *Unity and Diversity in Federal Systems*. Montreal: McGill-Queen's University Press, 2010. 109–38.

Gagnon, Alain-G., and James Tully, eds. *Multinational Democracies*. Cambridge: Cambridge University Press, 2001.

Gagnon, Alain-G., Luc Turgeon, with Olivier De Champlain. "La bureaucratie représentative au sein des états multinationaux." *Revue française d'administration publique* 2, no. 118 (2006), 291–306.

Gagnon, Bernard, ed. *La diversité québécoise en débat: Bouchard, Taylor et les autres*. Montreal: Québec Amérique, Débats collection, 2010.

Gervais, Stéphan, Dimitrios Karmis, and Diane Lamoureux, eds. *Du tricoté serré au métissé serré? La culture publique commune au Québec en débats*. Quebec: Les Presses de l'Université Laval, 2008.

Ghai, Yash, ed. *Autonomy and Ethnicity: Negotiating Competing Claims in Multi-Ethnic States*. Cambridge: Cambridge University Press, 2000.

Gilley, Bruce. *The Right to Rule: How States Win and Lose Legitimacy*. New York: Columbia University Press, 2009.

Giner, Salvador, Llufs Raquer, Jordi Busquet, and Nûria Bultà. *La cultura catalana: El sagrat i el profà*. Barcelona: Éditions 16, 1996.

Goldenberg, Eddie. *The Way it Works: Inside Ottawa*. Toronto: Douglas Gibson Books, 2006.

González, Antoni Muñoz, and Josep Catà i Tur. *Absolutisme contre pactisme: La ciutadella de Barcelona (1640–1704)*. Barcelona: Rafael Dalmau Editor, 2008.

Government of Canada. *Report of the Royal Commission on Bilingualism and Biculturalism, Book III, The Work World*. Ottawa: Queen's Printer, 1969.

Government of Nunavut. *Inuit Language Protection Act: Backgrounder*. http://www.gov.nu.ca/news/2008/september/sept19a.pdf.

Grammond, Sébastien, *Aménager la coexistence. Les peuples autochtones et le droit canadien*. Brussels/ Montreal: Bruylant/Éditions Yvon Blais, 2003.

Greer, Scott L. *Nationalism and Self-Government: The Politics of Autonomy in Scotland and Catalonia*. Albany: State University of New York Press, 2008.

Guibernau, Montserrat. *Catalan Nationalism: Francoism, Transition and Democracy*. London: Routledge, 2004.

Guibernau, Montserrat. *The Identity of Nations*. Cambridge: Polity Press, 2007.

Guibernau, Montserrat. "Nations without States: Political Communities in the Global Age." *Michigan Journal of International Law* 25, no. 4 (2004).

Guibernau, Montserrat. *Nations without States: Political Communities in a Global Age*. Cambridge: Polity Press, 1999.

Guibernau, Montserrat. *Per un catalanisme cosmopolita*. Barcelona: Angle Editorial, 2009.

Guillaume, Stéphane. *La question du Tibet en droit international*. Paris: L'Harmattan, 2009.

Guntermann, Éric. "La résistance au nationalisme linguistique: Une comparaison entre le Québec et la Catalogne." Master's thesis, Institut d'Études Politiques de Paris, 2009.

Gutiérrez Chong, Natividad, ed. *Estados y autonomias en democracias contemporaneas*. Mexico: Plaza y Valdés, 2008.

Hagège, Claude. *Halte à la mort des langues*. Paris: Odile Jacob, 2000.

Hardy, Henry, ed. *Liberty*. Oxford: Oxford University Press, 2002.

Hechter, Michael. *Internal Colonialism: The Celtic Fringe in British National Development*. London: Routledge and Kegan Paul, 1975.

Henders, Susan J. *Territoriality, Asymmetry, and Autonomy: Catalonia, Corsica, Hong Kong, and Tibet*. London: Palgrave Macmillan, 2010.

Henderson, James Youngblood. "Dialogical Governance: A Mechanism of Constitutional Governance." *Saskatchewan Law Review* 72, no. 1 (2009), 153–61.

Henderson, Sakej. "Empowering Treaty Federalism." *Saskatchewan Law Review* 58, no. 2 (1994), 271–315.

Herrero de Minon, Miguel. *Derechos historicos y constitucion*. Madrid: Tecnos, 1998.

Herrero de Minon, Miguel. "Pactismo y nacionalismo inclusivos." In Jon Arrieta and Jesus Astigarraga, eds, *Conciliar la diversidad: Pasado y presente de la vertebracion de Espana*. Bilbao: Editorial de la Universidad del Pais Vasco, 2009. 233–8.

Himmelfarb, Gertrude, ed. *Essays on Freedom and Power*. Glencoe: The Free Press, 1949.

Hudon, Marie-Ève. *Language Regimes in the Provinces and Territories*. Ottawa: Legal and Legislative Affairs Division, Parliamentary Information and Research Service, Library of Parliament, 20 July 2011. http://www.parl.gc.ca/Content/LOP/ResearchPublications/2011-66-e.pdf.

Hueglin, Thomas. "From Constitutional to Treaty Federalism: A Comparative Perspective." *Publius* 30, no. 4 (2000), 137–63.

Hume, David. *Essays, Moral and Political*. London: Printed for A. Millar and A. Kincaid in Edinburgh, 1748.

Ignatieff, Michael. *The Rights Revolution*. Toronto: Anansi, 2000.

Innerarity, Daniel. *Éthique de l'hospitalité*. Quebec: Les Presses de l'Université Laval, 2009.

Innerarity, Daniel. *The Future and Its Enemies: In Defense of Political Hope*. Stanford, CA: Stanford University Press, 2012.

Innerarity, Daniel. *The Transformation of Politics: Governing in the Age of Complex Societies*. Brussels: Peter Lang, 2010.

Inuit Language Protection Act, SNu 2008, c. 17. http://www.canlii.org/en/nu/laws/stat/snu-2008-c-17/latest/snu-2008-c-17.html.

Jaumain, Serge, ed. *La réforme de l'État … et après? L'impact des débats institutionnels en Belgique et au Canada*. Brussels: Éditions de l'Université de Bruxelles, 1997.

Jennar, Raoul Marc. "Ces accords que Bruxelles impose à l'Afrique: Une Europe toujours à construire." *Le monde diplomatique*, February 2005, 10.

Jennar, Raoul Marc. *Europe, la trahison des élites*. Paris: Fayard, 2004.

Jenson, Jane. "Recognising Difference: Distinct Societies, Citizenship Regimes and Partnership." In Guy Laforest and Roger Gibbins, eds, *Beyond the Impasse, Toward Reconciliation*. Montreal: Institute for Research on Public Policy, 1998.

Jenson, Jane, and Susan Phillips. "Regime Shift: New Citizenship Practices in Canada." *International Journal of Canadian Studies* 14, Fall (1996), 111–36.

Juliana, Enric. "El respeto." *La Vanguardia*, 28 November 2009, 15.

Kant, Immanuel. *Critique of Judgment*. New York: Hafner Publishing Company, 1951.

Karmis, Dimitrios. "Pourquoi lire Proudhon aujourd'hui? Le fédéralisme et le défi de la solidarité dans les sociétés divisées." *Politique et Sociétés* 21, no. 1 (2002), 43–65.

Karmis, Dimitrios, and Alain-G. Gagnon. "Fédéralisme et identités collectives au Canada et en Belgique: Des itinéraires différents, une fragmentation similaire." *Revue canadienne de science politique* 29, no. 3 (1996), 435–68.

Karmis, Dimitrios, and Jocelyn Maclure. "Two Escape Routes from the Paradigm of Monistic Authenticity: Post-Imperialist and Federal Perspectives on Plural and Complex Identities." *Ethnic and Racial Studies* 24, no. 3 (2001), 361–85.

Karmis, Dimitrios, and Wayne Norman, eds. *Theories of Federalism: A Reader*. London: Palgrave Macmillan, 2005.

Karmis, Dimitrios, and François Rocher, eds. *La dynamique confiance/méfiance dans les démocraties multinationales: Sous l'angle comparatif*. Quebec: Les Presses de l'Université Laval, 2012.

Katzenstein, Peter. *Small States in World Markets: Industrial Policy in Europe*. Ithaca: Cornell University Press, 1985.

Kaufmann, Eric P., ed. *Rethinking Ethnicity: Majority Groups and Dominant Minorities*. London: Routledge, 2004.

Keating, Michael. *The Independence of Scotland: Self-Government and the Shifting Politics of Union*. Oxford: Oxford University Press, 2009.

Keating, Michael. *Nations against the State: The New Politics of Nationalism in Quebec, Catalonia and Scotland*. 2nd edition. Basingstoke: Palgrave Macmillan, 2001.

Keating, Michael. *Plurinational Democracy: Stateless Nations in a Post-Sovereignty Era*. Oxford: Oxford University Press, 2001.

Keating, Michael, and John McGarry, eds. *Minority Nationalism and the Changing International Order*. Oxford: Oxford University Press, 2001.

Kelly, James B., and Christopher Manfredi. *Contested Constitutionalism*. Vancouver: UBC Press, 2009.

Kincaid, John. "Introduction to the Handbook of Federal Countries." Forum of Federations. http://www.forumfed.org/en/federalism/introduction tohandbook.php.

Klebes, Heinrich. "Projet de protocole additionnel de l'Assemblée parlementaire à la Convention européenne pour la protection des minorités nationals." *Revue universelle des droits de l'homme* 5, nos. 5–6 (1993).

Klein, Juan-Luis, and Benoît Lévesque, eds. *Contre l'exclusion: Repenser l'économie*. Quebec: Les Presses de l'Université du Québec, 1995.

Kunz, Josef L. "The Meaning and the Range of the Norm Pacta Sunt Servanda." *American Journal of International Law* 39, no. 2 (1945), 180–97.

Kymlicka, Will. *Finding Our Way: Rethinking Ethnocultural Relations in Canada*. Oxford: Oxford University Press, 1998.

Kymlicka, Will. "Misunderstanding Nationalism." *Dissent*, Winter (1995), 130–7.

Kymlicka, Will. *Multicultural Citizenship: A Liberal Theory of Minority Rights*. Oxford: Oxford University Press, 1995.

Kymlicka, Will. *Multicultural Odysseys: Navigating in the New International Politics of Diversity*. Oxford: Oxford University Press, 2007.

Lachapelle, Guy, ed. *Diversité culturelle, identités et mondialisation: De la ratification à la mise en oeuvre de la convention sur la diversité culturelle*. Quebec: Les Presses de l'Université Laval, 2008.

Laforest, Guy. "Articuler une pensée fédéraliste authentique au Québec." *Recherches sociographiques* 57, no. 2 (2006), 345–53.

Laforest, Guy. *De la prudence*. Montreal: Boréal, 1993.

Laforest, Guy. *Pour la liberté d'une société distincte: Parcours d'un intellectuel engage*. Quebec: Les Presses de l'Université Laval, 2004.

Laforest, Guy, and Roger Gibbins, eds. *Beyond the Impasse, Toward Reconciliation*. Montreal: Institute for Research on Public Policy, 1998.

Lajoie, Andrée. "Federalism in Canada: Provinces and Minorities – Same Fight." In Alain-G. Gagnon, ed., *Contemporary Canadian Federalism*. Toronto: University of Toronto Press, 2009. 183–209.

Lajoie, Andrée. *Le pouvoir déclaratoire du Parlement: Augmentation discrétionnaire de la compétence fédérale au Canada*. Montreal: Les Presses de l'Université de Montréal, 1969.

Laponce, Jean. *Languages and Their Territories*. Toronto: University of Toronto Press, 1987.

LaSelva, Samuel V. *The Moral Foundations of Canadian Federalism: Paradoxes, Achievements, and Tragedies of Nationhood*. Montreal: McGill-Queen's University Press, 1996.

Latouche, Daniel. "Le pluralisme ethnique et l'agenda public au Québec." *Revue internationale d'action communautaire* 21 (1989), 11–23.

Leclair, Jean. "The Supreme Court of Canada's Understanding of Federalism: Efficiency at the Expense of Diversity." *Queen's Law Journal* 28 (2003), 411–53.

Lecours, André, and Geneviève Nootens, eds. *Dominant Nationalism, Dominant Ethnicity: Identity, Federalism and Democracy*. Brussels: Les Presses interuniversitaires européennes/Peter Lang, 2009.

Legaz y Lacambra, Luis, et al. *El pactismo en la Historia de España*. Madrid: Instituto de España, 1980.

Levine, Marc. *The Reconquest of Montreal: Language Policy and Social Change in a Bilingual City*. Philadelphia: Temple University Press, 1991.

Lijphart, Arend. *Democracies: Patterns of Majoritarian and Consensus Government in Twenty-One Countries*. New Haven: Yale University Press, 1984.

Lijphart, Arend. *Democracy in Plural Societies: A Comparative Exploration*. New Haven: Yale University Press, 1977.

Lijphart, Arend. *Thinking about Democracy: Power Sharing and Majority Rule in Theory and Practice*. London: Routledge, 2008.

Linz, Juan L. *Democracy, Multinationalism and Federalism*. Instituto Juan March de Estudios e Investigaciones, Working paper 103, June 1997.

Lustick, Ian. "Stability in Deeply-Divided Societies: Consociationalism versus Control." *World Politics* 31, no. 3 (1979), 325–44.

Lutz, Ellen, Hurst Hannum, and Kathryn J. Burke, eds. *New Directions in Human Rights*. Philadelphia: University of Pennsylvania Press, 1989.

MacCormick, Neil. *Questioning Sovereignty: Law, State, and Nation in the European Commonwealth*. Oxford: Oxford University Press, 1999.

McEwen, Nicola. *Nationalism and the State: Welfare and Identity in Scotland and Quebec*. Brussels: Peter Lang, 2006.

McGarry, John, and Michael Keating, eds. *Nations, Minorities and European Integration*. London: Routledge, 2006.

McRae, Kenneth D. "Bilingual Language Districts in Finland and Canada: Adventures in the Transplanting of an Institution." *Canadian Public Policy* 4, no. 3 (1978), 331–51.

McRae, Kenneth D. "The Principle of Territoriality and the Principle of Personality in Multilingual States." *International Journal of the Sociology of Language* 4 (1975), 35–54.

McRoberts, Kenneth. *Catalonia: Nation-Building without a State*. Toronto: Oxford University Press, 2001.

McRoberts, Kenneth. "Cultures, Language, and Nations: Conceptions and Misconceptions." Unpublished paper presented to the Sixteenth Annual London Conference for Canadian Studies, Birkbeck College, University of London, 26 February 2000, p. 25. http://www.mrifce.gouv.qc.ca/calendrier/document/614_McRoberts.pdf.

McRoberts, Kenneth. *Misconceiving Canada: The Struggle for National Unity*. Toronto: Oxford University Press, 1997.

Magord, André. *The Quest for Autonomy in Acadia*. Brussels: Les Presses interuniversitaires européennes/Peter Lang, 2008.

Máiz, Ramón. *The Inner Frontier: The Place of Nation in the Political Theory of Democracy and Federalism*. Brussels: Peter Lang, Diversitas collection, 2012.

Máiz, Ramón, ed. *Teorias Politicas Contemporaneas*. 2nd edition. Valencia: Tirant lo Blanch, 2009.

Máiz, Ramón, and Ferran Requejo, eds. *Democracy, Nationalism and Multiculturalism*. London: Routledge, 2005.

Marmen, Louise, and Jean-Pierre Corbeil. *Nouvelles perspectives canadiennes: Les langues au Canada, Recensement de 2001*. Quebec: Ministère des Travaux publics et Services gouvernementaux. 2004.

Martel, Angéline. "La politique linguistique canadienne et québécoise: Entre stratégies de pouvoir et d'identités." *Globe: Revue internationale d'études québécoises* 2, no. 2 (1999), 1–26.

Mason, Andrew. *Community, Solidarity and Belonging: Levels of Community and Their Normative Significance*. Cambridge: Cambridge University Press, 2000.

Millard, David. *Secession and Self: Quebec in Canadian Thought*. Montreal: McGill-Queen's University Press, 2008.

Miller, James R. *Compact, Contract, Covenant: Aboriginal Treaty-Making in Canada*. Toronto: University of Toronto Press, 2009.

Montpetit, Éric. *Le fédéralisme d'ouverture: La recherche d'une légitimité canadienne au Québec*. Quebec: Septentrion, 2007.

Moreno, Luis. *The Federalization of Spain*. London: Cass, 2001.

Moreno, Luis, and César Colino Cámara, eds. *Unity and Diversity in Federal Systems*. Montreal: McGill-Queen's University Press, International Project: A Global Dialogue on Federalism, Forum of Federations, 2010.

Morin, Claude. *Le pouvoir québécois en négociation*. Montreal: Les Éditions du Boréal Express, 1972.

Morin, Jacques-Yvan, and José Woehrling. *Demain, le Québec: Choix politiques et constitutionnels d'un pays en devenir*. Quebec: Septentrion, 1994.

Mouffe, Chantal. *Dimensions of Radical Democracy: Pluralism, Citizenship, Community*. London: Verso, 1992.

Niosi, Jorge. *La bourgeoisie canadienne: La formation et le développement d'une classe dominante*. Montreal: Boréal Express, 1979.

Noiriel, Gérard. *La tyrannie du national*. Paris: Calmann-Lévy, 1991.

Nordlinger, Eric. *Conflict Regulation in Divided Societies*. Cambridge, MA: Harvard University Press, 1972.

Norman, Wayne. *Negotiating Nationalism: Nation-Building, Federalism and Secession in the Multinational State*. Oxford: Oxford University Press, 2006.

Office of the Commissioner of Official Languages, Annual Report Special Edition, 35th Anniversary 1969–2004, vol. 1. http://epe.lac-bac.gc.ca/100/201/301/ra_commissaire_langues/html/ra04/v1/2004_05_e.htm.

Official Languages Act, 1968–1969, S.R.C. 1970, ch. 0–2, art. 2.

O'Leary, Brendan. "An Iron's Law of Nationalism and Federation? A (Neo-Diceyan) Theory of the Necessity of a Federal Staatsvolk, and a Constitutional Rescue." *Nations and Nationalism* 7 no. 3 (2001), 273–96.

Olling, R.D., and M.W. Westmacott, eds. *Perspectives on Canadian Federalism*. Scarborough: Prentice-Hall, 1988.

O'Neal, Brian, Alex Smith, and Jack Stilborn (prepared by). "The Gomery Commission Report Phase 2." Library of Parliament, 16 February 2006. http://www.parl.gc.ca/Content/LOP/ResearchPublications/prb0560-e.htm.

Orban, Edmond. *La dynamique de centralisation dans l'État fédéral. Un processus irréversible?* Montreal: Québec Amérique, 1984.

Palermo, Francesco. "When the Lund Recommendations Are Ignored: Effective Participation of National Minorities through Territorial Autonomy." *International Journal on Minority and Group* 16 (2009), 1–11.

Pammett, Jon H., and Christopher Dorman, eds. *The Canadian General Election of 2004*. Toronto: Dundurn Press, 2004.

Paquin, Stéphane. *La revanche des petites nations: Le Québec, l'Écosse et la Catalogne face à la mondialisation*. Montreal: VLB éditeur, 2001.

Paquin, Stéphane, ed. *Les relations internationales du Québec depuis la doctrine Gérin-Lajoie (1965–2005)*. Quebec: Les Presses de l'Université Laval, 2006.

Parekh, Bhikhu C. *The Future of Multi-Ethnic Britain: Report of the Commission of the Future of Multi-Ethnic Britain* (Parekh Report). London: Profile Books, 2000.

Parent, Christophe. *Le concept d'état fédéral multinational: Essai sur l'union des peuples*. Brussels: Les Presses interuniversitaires européennes/Peter Lang, Diversitas collection, 2011.

Patton, Paul, Duncan Ivison, and Douglas Saunders, eds. *Political Theory and Indigenous Rights*. Cambridge: Cambridge University Press, 2000.

Peleg, Ilan. *Democratizing the Hegemonic State: Political Transformation in the Age of Identity*. Cambridge: Cambridge University Press, 2007.

Pelletier, Réjean. *Le Québec et le fédéralisme canadien: Un regard critique*. Quebec: Les Presses de l'Université Laval, 2008.

Pettit, Philip. *Republicanism: A Theory of Freedom and Government*. Oxford: Oxford University Press, 1997.

Preliminary Report of the Royal Commission on Bilingualism and Biculturalism. Ottawa: Queen's Printer, 1965.

Prieto de Pedro, Jesus. *Cultura, Culturas y Constitucion*. Madrid: Centro de Estudios Politicos y Constitucionales, 2006 [1992].

Proudhon, Pierre-Joseph. "Du principe federative." In *Oeuvres complètes*, volume *Du principe fédératif. La fédération et l'unité en Italie. Nouvelles observations sur l'unité italienne. France et Rhin*. Paris: Marcel Rivière, 1959.

Quesada, Fernando, ed. *Estado plurinacional y ciudadania: Constitucionalismo y cuestion nacional*. Madrid: Editorial Biblioteca Nueva, 2003.

Rawls, John. *A Theory of Justice*. Cambridge, MA: Harvard University Press, 1971.

Raynauld, André, Gérald Marion, and Richard Béland. "The Distribution of Income in Canada among Ethnic Groups." Research Report prepared for the Royal Commission on Bilingualism and Biculturalism, 1966.

Reference regarding the secession of Québec, [1998] 2 R.C.S. 217. http://www.canlii.org/en/ca/scc/doc/1998/1998canlii793/1998canlii793.pdf

Renaut, Alain. *Un humanisme de la diversité: Essai sur la décolonisation des identités*. Paris: Flammarion, 2009.

Requejo, Ferran. "Cultural Pluralism, Nationalism, and Federalism: A Revision of Democratic Citizenship in Plurinational States." *European Journal of Political Research* 35, no. 2 (1999), 255–86.

Requejo, Ferran. "L'estat de les autonomies, 25 anys desprès." *Nous Horitzons* 175 (2004), 16–20.

Requejo, Ferran. *Federalisme plurinacional i estat de les autonomies: Aspects teorics i aplicats*. Barcelona: Proa, 2003.

Requejo, Ferran. "Hacia la independencia." *La Vanguardia*, 7 June 2010.

Requejo, Ferran. *Multinational Federalism and Value Pluralism: The Spanish Case*. London: Routledge, 2005.

Requejo, Ferran. *Pluralisme i autogovern al mon: Per unes democràcies de qualitat*. Vic: Editorial Eumo/Universitat de Vic, 2005.

Requejo, Ferran, ed. *Democracy and National Pluralism*. London: Routledge, 2001.

Resnick, Philip, and Daniel Latouche. *Letters to a Québécois Friend*. Montreal: McGill-Queen's University Press, 1990.

Ridao, Joan. *Les contradiccions del catalanisme i altres qüestions del laberint nacional*. Barcelona: L'esfera dels llibres, 2005.

Riedel, Sabine. "Minorités nationales en Europe et protection des droits de l'homme: Un enjeu pour l'élargissement." *Politique étrangère* 3 (2002), 647–64.

Rocher, François, et Benoît Pelletier, eds. *Le nouvel ordre constitutionnel canadien: Du rapatriement de 1982 à nos jours*. Quebec: Les Presses de l'Université du Québec, Politeia collection, 2013.

Royal Commission on Aboriginal Peoples (Erasmus-Dussault). *Final Report: Restructuring the Relationship*, volume 2. Ottawa: Groupe Communications Canada, 1996. See http://www.collectionscanada.gc.ca/webarchives/2007 1124125001/http://www.ainc-inac.gc.ca/ch/rcap/sg/sh1_e.html.

Ruiz Fabri, Hélène. "Maîtrise du territoire et rôle international de l'État." *Revue de l'Académie des sciences morales et politiques*, no. 1 (2000).

Rupesinghe, Kumar, and Valery A. Tishkov, eds. *Ethnicity and Power in the Contemporary World*. Tokyo: United Nations University Press, 1996. http://www.unu.edu/unupress/unupbooks/uu12ee/uu12ee00.htm.

Russell, Peter. "Trust and Distrust in Canada's Multinational Constitutional Politics." Workshop, Groupe de recherche sur les sociétés plurinationales, 4 June 2010.

Ryan, Claude. "The Agreement on the Canadian Social Union as Seen by a Quebec Federalist." In Alain-G. Gagnon and Hugh Segal, eds, *The Canadian Social Union: 8 Critical Analyses*. Montreal: McGill-Queen's University Press, 2000. 209–26.

Sabourin, Conrad, and Julie Bernier. *Government Responses to Language Issues: Canadian Examples*. Office of the Language Commissioner of Nunavut, 2001.

Safran, William, and Ramón Maíz, eds. *Identity and Territorial Autonomy in Plural Society*. London: Frank Cass, 2000.

Saint-Germain, Maurice. *Une économie à libérer: Le Québec analysé dans ses structures économiques.* Montreal: Les Presses de l'Université de Montréal, 1973.

Saiz Arnaiz, Alejandro. *Estado federal i estatuto particular: la posicion constitucional de la provincia de Quebec en la federacion canadiense.* Madrid: Instituto Vasco de Administracion Publica, 1997.

Salée, Daniel. "Enjeux et défis de l'affirmation identitaire et politique des peuples autochtones au Canada: Autour de quelques ouvrages récents." *Journal of Canadian Studies* 26, Fall (2002), 139–61.

Sanchez-Prieto, Juan María. "Mémoire de l'histoire et identité politique dans l'Espagne contemporaine." *Politeia. Cahiers de l'Association française des auditeurs de l'Académie internationale de droit constitutionnel* 6 (2004), 339–56.

Seidle, Leslie F., ed. *Seeking a New Canadian Partnership: Asymmetrical and Confederal Options.* Montreal: Institute for Research on Public Policy, 1994.

Seymour, Michel. *De la tolérance à la reconnaissance.* Montreal: Boréal, 2008.

Seymour, Michel. *Le pari de la démesure: L'intransigeance canadienne face au Québec.* Montreal: L'Hexagone, 2001.

Seymour, Michel. *États-nations, multinations et organisations supranationales.* Montreal: Liber, 2002.

Seymour, Michel, ed. *Nationalité, citoyenneté et solidarité.* Montreal: Liber, 1999.

Seymour, Michel, ed. *The Plural States of Recognition.* Basingstoke: Palgrave Macmillan, 2010.

Seymour, Michel, ed. "La politique de la reconnaissance et la théorie critique." *Politique et Sociétés* 28, no. 3, special edition (2009).

Seymour, Michel, ed. *La reconnaissance dans tous ses états: repenser les politiques de pluralisme culturel.* Montreal: Québec Amérique, Débats collection, 2009.

Seymour, Michel, and Alain-G. Gagnon, eds. *Multinational Federalism: Problems and Prospects.* Basingstoke: Palgrave Macmillan, 2012.

Skurbaty, Zelim. *Beyond a One-Dimensional State: An Emerging Right to Autonomy?* Leiden: Martinus Nijhoff, 2008.

Smiley, Donald, and Ronald L. Watts. *Intrastate Federalism in Canada.* Vol. 39, Research Studies, Royal Commission on the Economic Union and Development Prospects for Canada (Macdonald commission). Ottawa: Government Publishing Centre, Supply and Services Canada, 1985.

Smith, Anthony D. *Nations and Nationalism in a Global Era.* Cambridge: Polity Press, 1995.

Snyder, Louis L. *Macro-Nationalisms: A History of the Pan-Movements.* Westport, CT: Praeger, 1984.

Snyder, Louis L. *The Meaning of Nationalism.* New Brunswick, NJ: Rutgers University Press, 1954.

Sondage Léger Marketing. "L'opinion des Québécois à l'égard d'une Constitution du Québec." www.cyberpresse.ca.

Sonntag, Selma K. "La diversité linguistique et la mondialisation." *Politique et Sociétés* 29 (2010), 15–43.

Stevenson, Garth. *Parallel Paths: The Development of Nationalism in Ireland and Quebec*. Montreal: McGill-Queen's University Press, 2006.

Strange, Susan. *The Retreat of the State: The Diffusion of Power in the World Economy*. Cambridge: Cambridge University Press, 2000 [1996].

Suksi, Markku, ed. *Autonomy: Applications and Implications*. La Haye: Kluwer, 1998.

Taglioni, François. "Les revendications séparatistes et autonomistes au sein des territoires mono- et multi-insulaires: Essai de typologie." *Cahiers de géographie du Québec* 49, April (2005).

Tarling, Nicholas. *Historians and Southeast Asian History*. Auckland: New Zealand Asia Institute, University of Auckland, 2000.

Taylor, Charles. *Philosophy and the Human Sciences: Philosophical Papers 2*. Cambridge: Cambridge University Press, 1985.

Taylor, Charles. *Reconciling the Solitudes: Essays on Canadian Federalism and Nationalism*. Edited by Guy Laforest. Montreal: McGill-Queen's University Press, 1993.

Thériault, Joseph Yvon. *Faire société: Société civile et espaces francophones*. Sudbury, ON: Éditions Prise de parole, 2007.

Thomas, David. *Whistling Past the Graveyard: Constitutional Abeyance, Quebec and the Future of Canada*. Toronto: Oxford University Press, 1997.

Thomson, Dale C., ed. *Quebec: Society and Politics. A View from the Inside*. Toronto: McClelland & Stewart, 1973.

Tierney, Stephen. *Constitutional Law and National Pluralism*. Oxford: Oxford University Press, 2005.

Tierney, Stephen, ed. *Multiculturalism and the Canadian Constitution*. Vancouver: UBC Press, 2007.

Todorov, Tzvetan. *In Defense of the Enlightenment*. London: Atlantic Books, 2009.

Torres, Xavier. "Pactisme i patriotisme a la Catalunya de la Guerra dels Segadors." *Recerques* 32 (1995), 45–62.

Traisnel, Christophe. "Le nationalisme de contestation: Le rôle des mouvements nationalistes dans la construction politique des identités wallonne et québécoise en Belgique et au Canada." Doctoral dissertation, unpublished, Paris II–Université de Montreal, 2005.

Tremblay, André. "Federal Spending Power." In Alain-G. Gagnon and Hugh Segal, eds, *The Canadian Social Union: 8 Critical Analyses*. Montreal: McGill-Queen's University Press, 2000. 155–88.

Tsujimura, Miyoko, and Mari Osawa, eds. *Gender Equality in Multicultural Societies: Gender, Diversity, and Conviviality in the Age of Globalization*. Sendai: Tohoku University Press, 2010.

Tully, James. "Liberté et dévoilement dans les sociétés multinationals." *Globe, Revue internationale d'études québécoises* 2, no. 2 (1999), 13–36.

Tully, James. *Strange Multiplicity: Constitutionalism in an Age of Diversity.* Cambridge: Cambridge University Press, 1995.

Tully, James. *Public Philosophy in a New Key.* Vol. 1, *Democracy and Civic Freedom.* Cambridge: Cambridge University Press, 2008.

Tully, James. *Public Philosophy in a New Key.* Vol. 2, *Imperialism and Civic Freedom.* Cambridge: Cambridge University Press, 2008.

Turgeon, Luc. "La grande absente: La société civile au coeur des changements de la Révolution tranquille." *Globe, Revue internationale d'études québécoises* 2, no. 1 (1999), 35–56.

Turp, Daniel. *La nation bâillonnée: Le plan B ou l'offensive d'Ottawa contre le Québec.* Montreal: VLB éditeur, 2000.

Turp, Daniel. "Statut d'autonomie de la Catalogne – Un ordre constitutionnel imposé, comme au Québec." *Le Devoir,* 16 July 2010, A9.

Turp, Daniel (presented by). *Constitution québécoise,* Bill 196 (draft). 1st session, 38th Legislature. Quebec: Éditeur officiel du Québec, 2007.

United Nations. *United Nations Declaration on the Rights of Indigenous Peoples.* New York: United Nations, 2008.

Venice Commission. *Opinion on the Interpretation of Article 11 of the Draft Protocol to the European Convention on Human Rights Appended to Recommendation 1201 of the Parliamentary Assembly.* Venice: Council of Europe, 1996.

Viver i Pi-Sunyer, Carles. "Una deriva peligrosa del Tribunal Constitucional." *La Vanguardia,* 10 May 2010.

Waszek, Norbert. *L'Écosse des Lumières: Hume, Smith, Ferguson.* Paris: Les Presses universitaires de France, 2003.

Watts, Ronald. *Comparing Federal Systems.* Montreal: McGill-Queen's University Press, 2008.

Webber, Jeremy. *Reimagining Canada: Language, Culture, Community, and the Canadian Constitution.* Montreal: McGill-Queen's University Press, 1994.

Wences, Isabel. *Sociedad civil y virtud civica en Adam Ferguson.* Madrid: Centro de Estudios Politicos y Constitucionales, 2006.

Whitaker, Reginald. *A Sovereign Idea: Essays on Canada as a Democratic Community.* Montreal: McGill-Queen's University Press, 1992.

Widdowson, Frances, and Albert Howard. *Disrobing the Aboriginal Industry: The Deception behind Indigenous Cultural Preservation.* Montreal: McGill-Queen's University Press, 2008.

Wildsmith, Bruce H. "Treaty Responsibilities: A Co-Relational Model." *University of British Columbia Law Review* 26 (1992), 324–37.

Williams, Robert A., Jr. *Linking Arms Together: American Indian Treaty Vision of Law and Peace, 1600–1800.* London: Routledge,1999.

Wilson, V. Seymour. "The Tapestry Vision of Canadian Multiculturalism."
  Canadian Journal of Political Science 26, no. 4 (1993), 645–69.
Young, Iris Marion. *Inclusion and Democracy*. Oxford: Oxford University Press,
  2000.
Young, M. Crawford. *Revisiting Nationalism and Ethnicity in Africa*. Los Ange-
  les: Regents of the University of California, 2001.
Zapata-Barrero, Ricard, ed. *Immigration and Self-Government of Minority Na-
  tions*. Brussels: Peter Lang, Diversitas collection, 2009.

Name Index

Abu-Laban, Yasmeen, 51
Acton, John Emerich Edward, Lord, 96
Althusius, Johannes, 9

Barraqué, Jean Pierre, 84
Berlin, Isaiah, 14, 55–7, 70
Bhargava, Rajeev, 98
Blindenbacher, Raoul, 88
Bofill, Hector, 10
Boire, Roger, 6
Bouchard, Gérard, 34
Bouchard, Lucien, 79
Bourassa, Robert, 64, 79
Brouillet, Eugénie, 97
Burgess, Michael, 79, 85–6, 87–8

Cameron, David, 42
Caminal i Badia, Miquel, 6, 7, 86
Caron, Jean-François, 88
Charest, Jean, 66, 68
Chevrette, François, 58
Chevrier, Marc, 12
Choudhry, Sujit, 76
Chrétien, Jean, 60–1, 65
Clark, Joe, 11, 60
Conway, John, 97
Courchene, Thomas, 68

Dahl, Robert, 67
Davis, Rufus, 85
Dieckhoff, Alain, 3
Dion, Stéphane, 59
Duchacek, Ivo, 86

Eiximenis, Francesc, 85
Elazar, Daniel, 84, 86

Ferguson, Adam, 85
Flanagan, Tom, 92
Forbes, Donald, 49

García Calvo, Roberto, 101
Genovès, Dolors, 6
Gibbins, Roger, 82, 90
Goldenberg, Eddie, 61
Grammond, Sébastien, 91
Guibernau, Montserrat, 5

Hagège, Claude, 35
Harper, Stephen, 11, 66
Hechter, Michael, 5
Hume, David, 85, 97

Iacovino, Raffaele, 46
Ignatieff, Michael, 72
Innerarity, Daniel, 52, 76, 99, 100

Jennar, Raoul Marc, 36
Jenson, Jane, 39, 44, 82, 83
Juan Carlos, King of Spain, 101

Karmis, Dimitrios, 86, 89
Keating, Michael, 5
Kincaid, John, 84
Kingery, Sandra, 104
Kymlicka, Will, 12, 73–4, 82

Laforest, Guy, 53, 77, 82–3, 88, 90
Lajoie, Andrée, 57
Lamer, Antonio, Justice, 92
Laponce, Jean, 18
LaSelva, Samuel V., 86
Lesage, Jean, 63, 68
Lévesque, René, 25, 50, 63, 79
Lijphart, Arend, 76–7
Lindblom, Charles E., 67
Loughlin, John, 8
Lustick, Ian, 80

Martin, Paul, 65, 69
Marx, Herbert, 58
McGarry, John, 76
McRae, Kenneth D., 18
McRoberts, Kenneth, 5, 32, 82
Modood, Tariq, 94
Montesquieu, Charles-Louis de Secon-
    dat, 9, 96–7
Mulroney, Brian, 11, 60

Noël, Alain, 68, 82
Nootens, Geneviève, 49

O'Leary, Brendan, 76–8

Palermo, Francesco, 80
Parent, Christophe, 93
Parizeau, Jacques, 79

Pearson, Lester B., 60, 63
Pelletier, Benoît, 66, 68, 82
Pérez Tremps, Pablo, 101
Pettit, Philip, 14, 56–7
Phillips, Susan, 39
Pí i Margall, Francisco, 9
Proudhon, Pierre-Joseph, 7, 9

Rawls, John, 97
Renan, Ernest, 15
Renaut, Alain, 95, 97
Requejo, Ferran, 82, 86
Rocher, François, 82
Rodríguez Zapatero, José Luis,
    102
Roy, Jean-Pierre, 6

Schneiderman, David, 82–3
Seymour, Michel, 46, 97
Simeon, Richard, 76
Smith, Anthony, 9
Snyder, Louis, 4
Sonntag, Selma K., 16
Stasiulis, Daiva, 51
Stein, Janice, 42
Stendhal (Henri-Marie Beyle), 55

Taylor, Charles, 34, 51, 53, 57
Thériault, Joseph Yvon, 45
Tierney, Stephen, 47–8
Trudeau, Pierre Elliott, 24, 60
Tsujimura, Miyoko, 44
Tully, James, 9, 14, 47–8, 71, 78, 89,
    90–1
Turp, Daniel, 10

Vallières-Roland, Catherine, 88

Watts, Ronald, 87–8
Wilson, Vince, 51

Subject Index

abeyances, concept of, 48–9
Aboriginal peoples: aboriginal rights, 74, 76, 92; associations of, 90; dual citizenship, 91; federal policy toward, 91–2; merits of federalism to, 93. *See also* minority nations
accommodation policies, 76–8
Action démocratique du Québec, 63
active citizenship, 11, 13, 23, 45, 50, 52, 54, 67
Act of Quebec (1774), 4
Adeu, Espanya (Genovès), 6
African, Caribbean, and Pacific Group of States (ACP), 36
Ahwaz region, 74
allophones, 20–1, 24, 26
Austro-Hungarian Empire, 4, 12
autonomy: mechanism of enfranchisement, 14; negative and positive, 70–1; Quebec's claims of, 57, 63–4; study of, 80–1; territorial, 72–5, 80–1; territorial-cultural, 77–8

balance / imbalance of power, 57–9, 61–2, 70–1
balance in political societies, 96–7

Basque country, 8, 97, 103n1
Beyond the Impasse, Towards Reconciliation (Rocher and Schneiderman), 82–4, 93
bilingualism: in Canada, 18–21, 23–4; countries with official, 22; in New Brunswick, 28–9; personal, territorial, and institutional, 18–20; in public sector, 21, 24; in Quebec, 18, 21
Bill 6, a.k.a. Official Languages Act (Nunavut), 29
Bill 7, a.k.a. Inuit Language Protection Act (2008), 29–30
Bill 22, a.k.a. Official Language Act (Quebec), 25–6
Bill 101, a.k.a. Charter of the French Language (Quebec), 20, 26
Bloc Québécois, 65
Bouchard-Taylor Commission, 45, 47, 50, 52
Bouchard-Taylor Report, 44, 50
Bourassa government, 25, 64–5
British Columbia, 65
British North America Act (1867), 18

Canada: Aboriginal peoples, 91–2; acquisition of public properties,

58; balance of power in, 57–9; bilingualism, 18–21, 23–4; centre-periphery relations, 65–8 (*see also* Council of the Federation, The); citizenship building, 52; citizenship regimes, 39, 44; defiance of principle of moderation, 97; democracy, 47, 53–4; discrimination of French Canadians, 22; division of power and sovereignty, 68; federal culture, 12, 88–9; federal institutions, 67; government's power and jurisdiction, 57–8; knowledge of official languages, 19; language policy, 13, 16–18, 21–2, 24, 26, 32, 38; language regimes, 18, 20; minority rights, 20; multiculturalism, 51–2; as negotiated country, 57; "open federalism," 11; policy toward Quebec, 10, 41, 49–50, 59–60; studies of intercommunal relations, 32, 82–3

Canada-US Free Trade Agreement, 64

Canadian Social Union. *See* Social Union Framework Agreement (1999)

Catalonia: autonomous status, 5, 85; citizenship regime, 39; Constitutional Tribunal's decisions on status of, 5–6, 98–9, 101–4; economic prosperity, 30; idea of dignity, 98, 101–4; language policy, 17, 30–2; Linguistic Normalization Law, 31; national minorities, 6, 98–9; newspapers, 101; promulgation of active citizenship, 13–14; referendums, 8, 85, 99; relations with Quebec, 31; self-governance, 9–10; separatism, 8, 9; Statute of Autonomy, 48, 102

Charlottetown Accord (1992), 62, 64–5, 70

Charter of Rights and Freedoms (1982), 18, 20, 53; notwithstanding clause, 69

Charter of the French Language (Quebec), 20, 26

citizenship regimes, 13, 38–9, 40–5

conflict resolution, 87–8

Conservative Party of Canada, 60–1, 66

Constitution Act (1867), 53

Constitution Act (1982), 25–7, 44, 47–8, 57, 84

constitutionalism, 48, 53, 89, 90

Constitutional Tribunal of Spain, 5–6, 8, 98–9, 101, 103

containment and contentment strategies, 59–61, 64–5

Copenhagen Declaration (1990), 74

Cotonou Agreement (2000), 36

Council of Europe, 73–5

Council of the Federation, The, 68, 70

Court Challenges Program (CCP), 26–7

covenant, 84. *See also* pactism

Crimea, 74, 81

cultural pluralism, 67

declaratory power, 58

decolonization, 5

Democràcia Cuirassada (Bofill), 10

democracy: in Canada, 47, 53–4; federal culture and, 89; interculturalism and, 100; minority nations and, 5–6; pactism and, 89; study of, 76–7; threats to, 52–3

dignity, idea of, 94, 97–9, 101–4

dispute management, 90

diversity, 3, 76–8, 80, 96–7

East Timor, 9, 95
economic determinism, 37–8
Economic Partnership Agreements
(EPA), 36–7
empires, 4–5, 12
empowerment, 67, 69–70, 78, 80, 96
equality, 94
Erasmus-Dussault Commission, 91
European Convention on Human
Rights, 75
European Union, 31, 36–7
European Year of Intercultural Dia-
logue (2008), 44
Exploring Federalism (Elazar), 86

federal culture, 12, 15, 85–9
federalism: American model, 7, 86;
binational/multinational, 51; Canadian, 32, 51, 79, 83; in comparative perspective, 10; federal polity,
87–8; intra-state *vs.* inter-state, 66;
liberty and authority under, 6–7;
multinational, 12, 50–1, 73, 78–80;
nature and objectives, 16, 80; "open
federalism," 60; partnership systems as alternative to, 79; pluralist
federalism, 86–8, 90; promotion of
minority languages and, 32–3; as
response to globalization, 43; Supreme Court of Canada's interpretation of, 53; territorial, 51; by treaty,
15; views of, 79–80, 82–3, 85–6. *See
also* pactism; treaty federalism
federal paramountcy, 57
*Federal Principle: A Journey through
Time in Quest of Meaning, The*
(Davis), 85
First Nations. *See* Aboriginal peoples
First Nations? Second Thoughts (Flanagan), 92

Framework Convention for the
Protection of National Minorities,
The, 74
freedom. *See* liberty

Gendron Commission, 23, 25
globalization, 13, 34–7, 39, 95
Gomery Commission, 65
government of Canada, 57–61, 63, 67
Greenland, 6, 83

hospitality, principle of, 99–100

integration-accommodation dyad,
73, 77
integrationist strategy, 66–7, 69
integration policies, 77–8
inter-communal relations, 14–15,
50–1, 91, 99–100
interculturalism, 13–14, 49–52, 54, 100
international organizations, 95
Inuit Language Protection Act
(2008), 29–30
Iran, 74

Jacobin tradition in political philosophy, 8–9

Kosovo, 81, 95

La nation bâillonnée (Turp), 10
language policy: neoliberal view of,
38; in New Brunswick, 28–9; in
Nunavut, 17, 29–30; in Quebec,
17, 26–7
language regimes, 18, 20–1
legal pluralism, 82–3
Liberal Party of Canada, 60–1, 65, 67
liberty, 55–7, 95–6
linguistic bias, 16

linguistic diversity, 13, 35–7
linguistic rights, 18, 75

majority nations, 7, 71, 77, 79
Manitoba Act (1870), 18
Meech Lake Accord (1987), 48, 62, 64, 70
minority languages: accommodation of interests of, 78; allophone, 24; federalism and promotion of, 32–3; Inuit, 29–30
minority nations: challenges and threats to, 13–14, 41, 94–5; citizenship regimes and, 13; engagement in self-governance, 10–11; ethic of hospitality and, 76, 100; examples, 74; federalism and, 7; globalization and, 34, 41, 95; international organizations' policies toward, 73–5, 95; national emancipation, 3, 23, 78, 80; policy of exclusion, 41; principles for better treatment of, 81; prospects of survival, 3; recognition of, 5; self-identification, 14, 74; study of, 3–4, 70–3, 76–9, 80–1, 94–5; tensions with majority nations, 7
moderation, principle of, 96–7
Montreal, 21, 23
multiculturalism, 24–5, 49–52, 73
multinational federalism, 12, 14, 95–6
multinationalism, 25

national communities, 89
national diversity, 72
nationalism, 8
national minorities. See minority nations
nation building in Canada, 49–50

nation states: development of, 9–11; emergence of new, 4–5; erosion of Westphalian model of, 43; ethnocultural, 9. See also states
nations without states, 5
neoliberalism, 38
New Brunswick, 17, 18, 28–9
New Brunswick Confederation of Regions Party, 18
non-domination, 56
Nunavut, 17, 29–30

Office of the Commissioner of Official Languages report, 13
Official Language Act (Quebec), 25–6
Official Languages Act (1969), 20, 24
Official Languages Act (New Brunswick), 28
Official Languages Act (Nunavut), 29
Organization for Security and Cooperation in Europe (OSCE), 73, 75, 81
OSCE High Commissioner on National Minorities, 81

pacta sunt servanda, principle of, 98, 103
pactism, 15, 83–5, 89. See also federalism
Parekh Report, The, 44
Partido Popular (PP), 8, 99, 102
Partido Socialista Obrero Español (PSOE), 99
Parti Québécois (PQ), 25, 63, 65, 79
partnership systems, 79
"push and pull" policy, 21–2, 29, 32

Quebec: average income in, 17; bilingualism, 18, 21; Bouchard-Taylor Report, 44, 50; Canada's constitu-

tional reform and, 45–8; citizenship, 13–14, 39; commissions of
inquiry, 23, 45; Conservative Party
policies in, 60; containment policy
in, 59–60; criticism of Canadian
federalism in, 79; electoral reform
initiative, 45; empowerment
strategy, 69–70; identity, 45–6, 49,
65; immigration, 23, 27, 48, 64;
importance of treaty federalism
for, 92; informal constitution, 45,
47–9; institutional building, 45;
interculturalism, 46–52; international relations, 68; language
policy, 17, 20–7; language regime,
21; legislation, 22, 46; Liberal Party
policy in, 60–1; majority rights, 62;
opposition to Court Challenges
Program (CCP) in, 27; position on
multilateral agreements, 69–70;
referendums, 5, 62, 79; relations
with Catalonia, 31; relations with
central government, 64–6, 82–3;
self-governance, 9–10; separatism,
9, 41; status in Canadian federation, 46–8, 57; Supreme Court of
Canada's ruling on secession of,
9–10, 16–17
Quebec Charter of Human Rights
and Freedoms, 53
Quebec Liberal Party, 63–4, 66
Quebec Pension Plan, 63
Quebec's Quiet Revolution, 17
Questions nationales (Boire and Roy), 6

residual powers, 57
rights, individual and collective, 56
rival strategies, 72–3
Rowell-Sirois Commission, 69

Royal Commission on Bilingualism and Biculturalism, a.k.a. the
Laurendeau-Dunton commission,
20, 22, 24
Royal Commission on New Reproductive Technologies, 62

Scotland, 5–6, 9–10, 39
self-determination: domestic, 74;
idea of, 63, 76; policy, 66; principle
of, 81; right to, 93
self-rule, 62
separation of powers, 96–7
separatism, 49
shared rule, 62–3
Social Union Framework Agreement
(1999), 62, 65, 69, 70
Sommet de la Francophonie, 60
South Africa, 22
sovereignty, 51, 61–2, 68, 84–5
Soviet Union, 4
Spain: autonomies, 11, 85; challenges
to democracy, 101–2; Constitutional Tribunal ruling on Catalan
language, 31; nationalism and
sub-national movements, 97–8;
opposition to Catalan separatism,
8, 10; pactism, 85; political culture,
12; political parties, 99
state interventionism, 61
states: economic determinism of
modern, 38; freedom of nations
and limits of, 93; globalization
and erosion of, 35–6; Jacobin and
Girondin visions of, 8–9; newly
independent, 73; social investment
and neoliberal state, 42. See also
nation states
Summit of the Americas (2000), 41

Supreme Court of Canada: decision on language rights in New Brunswick, 28–9; *Reference re Secession of Quebec* (1998), 9–10, 16–17, 53, 62, 79
Switzerland, 12, 13, 22

Third World Network-Africa, 37
treaty federalism, 89–93. *See also* federalism

Ukraine, 81
UNESCO, 60
unilingualism, 18, 26
Union Nationale, 63
United Kingdom, 9, 12, 44

United Nations, 73; Human Development Programme Report, 95
United States of America, 64, 81
unity and liberty, 95–6

Van der Peet case, 92
Venice Commission, 75
Victoria Charter (1971), 64
"vivre-ensemble," 50

Wallonia, 39
White Paper on Intercultural Dialogue: Living Together as Equals in Dignity, 44
World Trade Organization (WTO), 36